꞉ ꞉ ꞉ ꞉ ꞉ ꞉ ꞉ ꞉

SIDMOUTH:

PRINTED FOR JOHN WALLIS, AT THE MA-RINE LIBRARY;

AND SOLD IN LONDON, BY

J. AND E. WALLIS, SKINNER STREET, SNOW HILL;

AND MESSRS. LONGMAN, HURST, AND CO.

PATERNOSTER BOW.

medication. TO THE *RESIDENT NOBILITY AND GENTRY,* AND TO THE VISITORS SID-MOUTH,

Cijijs 2i23orfc IS MOST RESPECTFUL-LY INSCRIBED.

BY THE PROPRIETOR,

JOHN WALLIS.

Sidmouth Marine Library. SIDMOUTH SCENERY. PART I. IN some situations, man is almost an amphibious animal: in warm climates he passes a great deal of his time in the water; and in all climates, at some seasons, to find ourselves plunged in the refreshing wave, and wrapped round with the liquid element, is a most delightful sensation. Health and pleasure are equally consulted in these salutary ablutions, and to many a wan countenance has the blush of the rose been restored by an occasional res-idence on the margin of the sea, and a frequent application of the purifying surge to the debilitated limb.

Extremes are often meeting in the his-tory of man. Savage and civilized life, in the case now under contemplation, produce, in a degree, the same effects. In the rude, and, what we at least term, the unpolished portions of our globe, the inhabitants are universally fond of bathing and swimming; indeed, they are accustomed to it from their earliest in-fancy, and consequently attain to a per-fection in aquatic exercises; and a ca-pacity of bearing them, if necessary, for a length of time, which the enfeebled children of civilization can seldom hope to equal: amongst them, however, tho

B same propensity to seek for health and gratification in the cooling or the tepid wave, has always been manifest-ed.

Imperial Rome, in the zenith of her glory, poured forth, every year, her nu-merous population to the shores of the Adriatic. Emperors and senators had their villas along the coast. By tempo-rary residences, from the vicinity of Naples, all round the borders of Cal-abria, the citizens of the mistress of the world, of all ages and ranks, sought a frequent renovation of that health which care and business had impaired, or more frequently, dissipation undermined.

The luxury and the wealth of Britain have produced the same effects. Within the last forty or fifty years, watering-places have been every year more and more the resort of the gay, the idle, and the valetudinary. From the extremities of the empire, and from the interior parts of our island, multitudes of per-sons are every season rushing to the coasts. Many of the formerly inconsid-erable towns and villages of it have thus been brought into notice; and, in almost all cases, accommodation and demand have kept pace with each other. The low, inconvenient cottage has given way to the lofty and spacious dwelling; and, instead of a little ale-house, the splendid inn has attracted the notice and supplied the wants of the visitant.

The West of England, almost every part of the coast of which has, in turn, been pronounced the Montpelier of the Island, abounds with these retreats from business, and cradles for the renovation of life.— Amongst the rest, Sidmouth is, every year, increasing its attractions, and as its means of accommodation are multiplied, receiving into its bosom a greater number of visitants and admir-ers.

The materials for the former histories of small and obscure places are, in gen-eral, very scanty. This is particularly the case with Sidmouth. The pen of history has no splendid fact to record, as having here taken place, nor has biography any distinguished name to select from its in-habitants. The writer of this account must, therefore, claim the indulgence of his readers, if they find it deficient in that interest and amusement which the records of many other places afford. All that can be done with respect to its former history, is to collect the *brief* notices of it, which are scattered in those histories of Devonshire which are already before the world, and add any circumstance which tradition has recorded, or which can be gleaned from MSS, or works upon other subjects, in which Sidmouth may be referred to. Ttisdon, Pole, and Polwhele, have been carefully consulted in drawing up this work. These, particularly the last, have examined all the preceding writers who have treated upon Devonshire and its inhabitants, and therefore, it may be presumed that nothing of any consequence can now be known respecting the former state of Sidmouth, but what is here brought together.

NAME AND SITUATION.

Sidmouth, anciently spelt Sidemew, is situated, as the name imports, near the spot where the small river Sid falls into the ocean. It lies nearly in the middle of thaf vast bay, which is bounded on the east by the Isle of Portland, and on the west by the Start Point. The whole of this extensive curve is scolloped with a number of hollows and small bays, formed by the bold headlands of Devon and Dorset. Between

B2 the lofty and magnificent ridges which these headlands terminate, a multitude of streams, which adorn and fertilize the rich vallies through which they flow, are continually finding their way to the great reservoir the sea. On the margin of one of these minor bays, bounded by Salcombe Hill on the east, and Peak Hill on the west, lies the small but rapidly-increasing subject of the present sketch.

By former writers, it is only noted as an "inconsiderable fishing-town." Leland says, " Sidmouth is a iisschar town, with a broke of that name, and a bay, six miles west of Seton; and Sir *W. Pole* writes, "Sidmouth, where the little river Sid runneth into the sea, is a small market town, and has been famous for fishing." Several persons are still living

who can attest the accuracy of such descriptions, and recollect almost the whole town consisting of thatched houses,'of dark stone, with their chimnies towards the street, a mode of building of which several specimens yet remain, and which still predominates in most of the unmodernized towns and villages of Devonshire.

Tradition reports, that here was formerly a harbour, which has been gradually choked up by accumulating sands. *Risdon,* in his "Survey of Devon," written in the reign of Charles II. gives this account: " Since the surrender to the Crown, Sidmouth is one of the chiefest fisher towns of this shire, and serveth much provision into the eastern parts, wherein her principal maintenance consists. But in times past, it was a port of some account, now choked with *chisel* and sands by the vicissitude of the tides. "

The rocks, which project for a considerable way from the shore, and extend almost across the whole of the Sidmouth bay, do not support this account, nor give much encouragement to a plan which has been suggested of forming an artificial harbour, by erecting a wall upon some of them, something like the "Cobb" at Lyme. Modern enterprize, however, we are witnesses, is capable of producing effects which had long been considered as dubious, at least, if not impracticable, and therefore, perhaps, some future period may witness the addition of an harbour to the growing accommodations of Sidmouth.

Not long ago, the public-spirited friends of the place, were flattered with the hope of seeing this desirable object accomplished. Towards the close of the year 1811, an Engineer was actually employed to make drawings, and estimate the expense of an harbour which it was proposed to form in a meadow called the *Ham,* through which the river Sid, flows into the sea. The necessary drawings and estimates being prepared, meetings were called upon the subject, and several gentlemen, among whom Sir Joseph Scott, Bart, particularly exerted himself, entered so warmly into the business, that at a general meeting

held at the London Inn, the following resolutions were unanimously adopted and published;

Sidmouth, Feb. 3, 1812. "At a meeting held this day at the London Inn, pursuant to the last adjournment, for the purpose of receiving the Engineer's estimate of the expenses attending the formation of an harbour in this town, it having been resolved unanimously, at a former meeting, that the same was feasible, and would be advantageous: Present i The Rev. William Jenkins. Sir Joseph Scott, Bart.

George Cornish, Esq. Francis Colman, Esq. Emanuel Baruh Lousada, Esq. Samuel Paul Paul, Esq. and upwards of fifty resident Gentlemen and Tradesmen in the town and neighbourhood. The following resolutions were entered into— 1. That Sir Joseph Scott, Bart. be requested to take the chair.

2. That Mr. Crocker's estimate, founded on Mr. Fawkner's plan, amounting to the sum of £15,352. 2 s. 11 d. having been submitted, be approved, and that the plan and estimate be left at the Library in this town, for public inspection. 3. That in case the plan be carried into effect, Mr. Charles Dalby be the contractor for the work.

Other resolutions to the number of twelve, follow, relative to the detail of the business, and the sum of £10,900, which was afterwards encreased to £11,800. was subscribed towards carrying it into execution.

It soon appeared that this plan would have powerful opponents—it was suggested that the western end of the beach afforded a more eligible situation for an Harbour, than that fixed upon by these resolutions—the friends of the design were divided, and as has, in a multitude of instances been the case, it was *lost* in a conflict between different and clashing interests!

FORMER TRADE.

It is certain that the former inhabitants of this place were largely engaged in the Newfoundland fishery, a branch of maritime commerce which now flourishes chiefly at Topsham, and at Poole, in Dorsetshire. By this lucrative, but frequently hazardous employment, many considerable, and some large fortunes have been accumulated—and to this, as well as our other fisheries and coal trade, we are indebted, in a great degree, for that breed of hardy and skilful mariners, to whose courage and dexterity our, islands are so deeply indebted, under Providence, for their safety from any hostile attack. Her navy has long been, and with the greatest reason, the boast of Britain: by this, even during the late terrible, protracted, and expensive war, the treasures of the most distant parts of the world were brought into our ports—an intercourse kept up with our numerous colonies—many of the foreign possessions of the enemy fell into our hands—and the greater part of those fleets which, in former periods, insulted and threatened us, even on our own shores, have been captured or destroyed. Such is the navy of Britain, and all possible attention ought to be paid it: but it may be permitted to the serious observer to remark, that there is a Higher Protection, which if we forfeit by national and individual iniquity, not all the navies or armies in the world can save us from destruction. That protection there is only one way of securing, and that is, not by noisy and hypocritical pretensions to piety; but by real, substantial, and persevering goodness of character.

MACKAREL CATCHING.

The fish with which Sidmouth is supplied, is but little pf it caught by the labours of an almost daily decreasing race of fishermen. The finny stores of the deep are brought in by boats, or by Jand carriage, from Beer on the east, and Brixham on the western side of this place Vast quantities of mackarel and whitings are occasionally caught, immediately opposite the town. They are taken in large nets called a *seine:* the origin of this name it does not appear possible to ascertain. The seine, and the boat, are worth an hundred pounds and upwards. The common seine is five hundred yards long; in the mackarel season they extend them to seven hundred, and even eight hundred yards. The boat having carried out the net to a certain distance, greater or less as circum-

stances may require, the seine is shot from the boat, which, as it moves on, forms a circle, being supported by a vast number of corks affixed, at equal distances, to the outside ropes of the net. From each end of the seine, when the semicircle is completed, are cords extending to the beach, and which are held by persons stationed to *haul* or putt in the seine, when completely cast into the sea: these individuals form two rows, which gradually close as the net approaches the shore. Many of the inhabitants and visitors of Sidmouth were gratified in the month of July 1809, with seeing above fifteen thousand mackarel brought in by *one* haul. It is a curious and entertaining sight to witness the beauty of this fish when first brought out of the water. The diversity and brightness of their colours, which vary every moment, cannot escape the most cursory observer. This is doubtless occasioned by the different atmosphere in which they are then placed? and humanity hopes that most of these are muscular motions, and speedily attended witli little pain to the expiring animal.

The produce of each *haul* is divided in the following manner: the owner of the seine and boat is entitled to one half of the fish caught; and also to an equal share of the remainder with the rest of the crew, between whom the other half is divided share and share alike. When women (which seldom happens at Sidmouth) take a part of the adventure, the supposed superiority of strength in the male quite supersedes that politeness which, in some other departments of society, pays a compliment to female assistance, for the lady gets only half as much as the gentleman.

Whether fish are taken or not, the labour is not over when the seine is pulled in. It is necessary that the net should be carefully *overhauled,* that is, spread regugarly out upon the shingles for drying; as, when it is first taken out of the sea, it is left in large hillocks, in which situation it would rot and not dry. This overhauling, after an unsuccessful shoot, is a very flat business—nearly an hour of toil is added, after the several labourers have found that there is not a

fish a-piece to repay them for their time and exertions. Soles, salmon-peal, red mullets, john-dories, turbot, pipers, gurnets, and brills, are the fish most commonly brought to Sidmouth. The shellfish are crabs, lobsters, shrimps, and prawns.

SIZE OF THE PARISH.

Sidmouth, in some old writings called *Sidmouth St. Nicholas,* is but a small parish; being only three miles in its greatest, and two miles in its shortest length, and about one mile in breath. It is bounded by Harpford and Sidbury on the north, by Salcombe Regis on the east, by the sea on the south, and by Otterton on the west. Farm-houses appear in several different parts of the parish, chiefly belonging to the manor of Sidmouth; they are built in general of cob, a composition-of clay and straw, (named probably from tlfe Greek, *Komrog,)* and stone, and have roofs of thatch. The farms are small, and each divided into a number of little fields, and mostly in a good state of cultivation.

Sidmouth, it is said, was a boroughtown in the 13th century. This report is certainly not contradicted by the following information, which is to be found in Sir *William Monson's* Naval Tracts: "In the fleet of eleven hundred sail, in the reign of King Edward III. the several ports were, upon forty days' warning, to furnish such a number of ships for fifteen days, upon their own charge, after setting sail; and to do it every year if demanded: the rest of the time the King to pay them." That Devon was then one of the most considerable maritime counties, appears from its sending from

Ships.	Mariners.
Seaton 2	25
Sidmouth 3	62
Exmouth 10	193
Teignmouth 7	120
Dartmouth 32	283
Plymouth 26	603
Yalme 2 47 82	1333
London, at that time, sent 25	662
Bristol 22	608
Yarmouth 43	950 MANOR.

The manor of Sidmouth was demised by indenture, under the seal of the monastery of Sion, to which it had been given in 1414, dated February 5, fourteenth of

Henry VIII. to Richard Gosnell, gentleman, for ninetynine years, under the yearly rent of £38. 7s. 8d. By old deeds it appears that the manor and rectory reserved to the crown after the dissolution, were, in the reign of Elizabeth, leased to Sir W. Peryam, knt. during his natural life. James I. let it to Christopher Manwaring, at the yearly rent £54. 7s. 8d. The manor was afterwards sold by Christopher Manwaring, esq. to Sir Edmond Prideaux, bart. and at the same time the great tythes were sold to Wadham-college. Sir Wilmot Prideaux was the owner of the manor in 1775; and held his court-leet and court-baron at Sidmouth. Thomas Jenkins, esq. then residing at Rome, became, by purchase, the next lord of the manor; and from him it came to his nephew, the present Thomas Jenkins, esq. When Brice wrote, he tells us, that at Sidmouth are "some respectable merchants, particularly the *Follets,* of good reputation for probity and honour," and till 1814, the name was preserved in the town, by the late Mr. *Abraham Follett,* who has left a large family.

GENERAL DESCRIPTION.

Sidmouth has a bold open shore, but, on account of the depth of the bay in which it lies, but few vessels of any magnitude come nearer than the extreme edge of the horizon. Fishing and pleasure boats are frequently seen spotting the deep blue of the ocean with their white sails, and affording, as they tack and shift their positions, a pleasing and interesting spectacle. Many of the newest lodging houses are ranged upon the beach, which is defended from the attacks of the ocean by a natural rampart of pebbles, which rises in four or five successive stages, from the surface of the sea, at low water. Wittt-every tide, the exterior parts of this shifting wall assume some different situation; are sunk either higher or lower; or are driven to the east or west, according to the strength and direction of-the wind. At low water, considerable spaces of fine hard sand are visible—these afford a walk, which would be more pleasant, were it not so

frequently interrupted by collections of stones, and streams, which find their way between the pebbles to their parent ocean. In dry weather, however, these streams are very inconsiderable.

At *lew* tides, a fine ride is to be obtained on the *sands* to the westward of Chit Rock; this road is equally practicable for pedestrians if defended by thick shoes.

As a watering-place, Sidmouth, in its natural advantages, yields to none, and exceeds many of those retreats of *Hygeia,* which utility and fashion have found out, on almost all the coasts of our island. An air mild and salubrious; a soil uncommonly fertile; the purest water, continually flowing; and a situation defended from every wind but the south, give it a pre-eminence over most of those places on our coasts, which are now so generally resorted te both for health and amusement. The beautiful vale in which the town stands is bounded on both sides by long lofty mountains; these form its eastern and western sides; and, towards the north, it is screened by the Gittisham and Honiton hills.

PLACES ON THE COAST.

That part of the coast which can be seen from Sidmouth beach, has been thus described: From the harbour of Dartmouth, the coast, winding to the northeast, shoots out into a promontory called Berry-head, which forms one side of Torbay, where is a good road for shipping, but, excepting Brixham, no port. Beyond this lies Teignmouth. Exmouth next appears in view, and then Sidmouth. Nor ought Seaton to be overlooked, once a capacious port, though at present an inconsiderable creek. A great part of the cliffs on the coast, from Exmouth to Lyme, are nearly four hundred feet high, and almost perpendicular. "The High-peak at Sidmouth is supposed to rise twelve hundred feet from the sea. Trom Hope's-nose to-the Berryhead is formed Torbay, being nearly a semicircle of twelve miles."

Changes more or less considerable are frequently taking place upon the coast. In the year 1788, there happened a remarkable slip of earth upon the

coast, about half a mile from Beer. From a pasture-down called Southdown, a great quantity of the cliff gave way, and sank down to a considerable depth. The plane surface was full six acres of good ground, and the depth measured perpendicularly about two hundred feet. It happened about twelve o'clock at night: the huge part of the cliff went off with a terrible noise, that greatly alarmed the people of Beer. A more than usual quantity of rain had fallen for many successive days before the cliff gave way. It is the washing of the sea, together with the action of the frosts and wind, which has formed the cliffs at Sidmouth; they were originally sloping hills, which, being gradually washed at the bottom, fell down.

One of these *looscnings* of the coast, as they are termed, took place in April 1, 181, just beyond that part of Peak-hill, on which the signal-house still stands: it has rendered the former road between Sidmouth and Exmouth so impassable, that the circuitous course which carriages and horses are now obliged to take has added two miles to the distance betwixt the two places. The road by Newton Poppleford, which is less hilly, is two miles further.

INTERNAL SCENERY.

From the *beach,* Sidmouth appears, on three sides of it, encompassed with hills; the tops of which, in a beautifully undulating line, form a vast curve of uncommon richness and simplicity. Cultivation nearly ascends to the summits of some of them; and the enclosures, which are numerous, present a rich variety of arable and pasture grounds. Where there are no enclosures, a short, sweet and darkish grass covers these elevations. Furze and heath, with their yellow and purple flowers, fill the air with fragrance, and beautifully diversify the scene. Great numbers of sheep browze upon this delicious herbage; and the cottages and bakers' ovens of the town and its vicinity are, many of them, supplied with fuel from these mountainous store-houses.

The hedges of Devonshire are proverbially large and rich. Sidmouth is closely surrounded with them like so many green and flowery zones. Elms, ashes, and oaks are interspersed in great numbers in almost every enclosure: these are the foresters most commonly to be met with, but many other sorts are scattered here and there. Orchards abound in all directions, and that agreeable beverage, cyder, is plentiful, and often extremely delicious. It is probably owing to the pigs being turned into the orchards when the young fruit is dropping from the trees, that a great deal of the Devonshire pork is peculiarly well flavoured.

In the vernal and autumnal parts of the year, the numerous lanes which intersect and divide this rich valley, are truly delightful. The country then seems a universal garden; the air is full of fragrance; and the eye gratified, almost beyond conception, with an incalculable diversity of shrubs and flowers: the deep banks are literally covered with vegetable mosaic. Trees, many of which are very lofty, as well as umbrageous, wave their rich foliage in the air, and almost on the margin of the sea display all the luxuriance of inland vegetation. Great quantities of holly and ivy enliven the dreary months of winter; and, with myrtles, laurels, and other evergreens, shed a perpetual verdure over this charming spot. In vallies there is seldom much flat surface: of this, Sidmouth vale is an example—slopes and swells every where meet the eye. Streams, so transparent as to reveal every pebble over which they flow, run from almost every declivity, soothe the ear with their murmurs, and refresh, as well as decorate, the landscape of which they form so sweet a part. The serpentine *Sid,* which, in still weather, is as clear as any of its neighbouring brooks, waters the whole eastern side of the valley, and, as it approaches the ocean, washes the marly rocks at the east end of the beach. In summer, this stream is so inconsiderable, as to have no *visible* communication with the sea; but in winter, or in any part of the year, when swollen by the rain, it becomes an impetuous torrent. It then disdains to creep between the pebbles, but driving them to the right hand and the left, opens for itself an unin-cumbered passage to the "great storehouse of the deep," and, from no inconsiderable *mouth,* pours into it, its freshning current.

THE TOWN

Consists of about three hundred houses and, in the census taken by order of Parliament in the year 1803, was said to contain twelve hundred and fifty-two inhabitants. This number, according to the census in 1813, was increased to above 1600. Beginning from what is termed Mill-cross, at the north end of the town, and ending at the beach, its length is about the third part of a mile. For rather more than half of this space it is, principally, one street; the remainder is divided into two branches like the letter Y. In the *eastern* branch, which seems rather the best of the two, are shops of almost every description, and two of the inns of the town, the *London Inn* and the *New Inn.* In the western branch of the main street is the Post-office. Both branches of the Y, as well as the main stem, contain lodging-houses, very various both in size and price.

At the London Inn commences a short cross street, which ends in the market-place. On the west of this is a division called *Western Town,* in which most of the remains of the old buildings of Sidmouth are to be found: it consists chiefly of poor low cottages, many of which will, probably, at the expiration of their present tenures, give place to buildings more suitable to those with which they are surrounded. On the east side of the town is another suburb, called, probably from its low situation, as it descends to the river, the *Marsh.* Here are also some lodging-houses, and, in the narrower part of it, towards the sea, many small residences for the poorer sort of people have lately been erected.

Returning again to the London Iitj, from thence, *a* small remaining part of the main street terminates at the beach.

RELIGION,

That bond of union between heaven and earth, that golden chain which connects man with his Maker, is, undoubtedly, a matter of the highest importance to mankind. This is a sentiment which, in all ages and countries, has been felt, and which is sanctioned, in the fullest manner, by the pages of inspired truth. Altars and temples, *around,* or *in* which mankind might, at stated times, unite in pouring out the pious effusions of gratitude, reverence, and humility, have appeared in all places—it is, therefore, but a proper homage paid to the religious principle, in attempting a description of any place, to begin with noticing those edifices which have been set apart for the public worship of God. This sentiment directs us to THE CHURCH.

This structure, which is supposed to be about four hundred years old, is a convenient place of worship. Both within and without, an air of neatness predominates. It is a slated stone edifice, and its tower is remarkably well built; its open windows are handsomely ornamented: the dial of the clock, which has been lately put up, obscures one of them—of this, some architectural antiquarians have complained, as a sacrifice of taste to utility; but, upon the principle that a "living *Religo,* Lat., *to bind, to make fast.*
C
dog is better than a dead lion," surely such an objection should be given up. A *clock,* which is of constant use to a whole town, is unquestionably of more value than a *window* in a steeple, which not above one person in five hundred would look at with any particular attention. The number of bells in this tower are five. The church had once an organ, which, we are told," was destroyed in Cromwell's days." It has not, however, now to lament the want of this appropriate piece of church music, as a small one has been lately erected by subscription. The south, or principal entrance, which has been lately repaired, and over it a new window opened, is surmounted by a small stone cross, similar to some, others at the angles of the roof. The claims of this edifice to the tutelage of a patron Saint, are divided, betwixt the rival names of St. *Nicholas* and St. *Giles.* The argument in favour of St. Nicholas, who is a sort of Christian Neptune, is, that many churches upon the Coast are dedicated to him, and

this, amongst the rest. *That,* in favour of St. Giles is, perhaps, rather stronger, which is, that the parish wake is held on St. Giles's Monday.

Amongst the older monuments in this church is one, on the north side of the chancel, to the memory of Walter Harlewin, Esq.; on the east another, to the memory of the Reverend John Miushull, formerly vicar of this parish; on the south, a third, in memory of the Reverend Oliver Courtrice, and John his son, the two preceding vicars. Of the modern mural records, many of which adorn both internally and externally the walls of this edifice, and commemorate the virtues of the dead, or hold out admonitory lessons to the living, one of the most distinguished preserves the memory of Dr. Currie of Liverpool; and another, that of a lady from Northumberland: both are slabs of white marble, and surmounted with urns. The inscription on the first of these is as follows:
To the memory of
James Currie, M.D. F.R.S.
late of Liverpool, afterwards of Bath, who died at this place August 31, 1805, aged 49 years.
The milder virtues which the friend endear,
The soften'd worth which makes affection's tear,
And all that brightens in life's social day,
Lost in the shades of death, may pass away:
Fast comes the hour when no fond heart shall know,
How lov'd, Oh, Currie, was the dust below.
Here cease the triumphs which the grave obtains,
The man may perish, but the sage remains.
Freedom and Peace shall tell to many an age,
Thy warning counsels, thy prophetic page:
Art, taught by thee, shall o'er the burning frame,
The healing freshness pour, and bless thy name:
And Genius, proudly while to Fame she turns,

Shall twine thy laurels with the wreath of Burns.

The inscription on the second monument above mentioned, and which is very near Dr. Currie, i& in these words, *on the urn:*
Mary
Wife of Robert Lisle of Acton-house, in the county of Northumberland, Esq. died 21 February 1791, aged 39 years, and, by her own desire, lies buried here. *(On the slab below:)*
Blest with soft airs from health-restoring skies,
Sidmoufh! to thee the drooping patient flics;
Ah! not unfailing is thy port to save,—
To her thou gav'st no refuge but a grave:
Guard it, mild Sidmouth, and revere its store,
More precious none shall ever touch thy shore.
C 2
Many appropriate texts of scripture, evidently painted a considerable time ago, are conspicuously placed in the body of the church.

A new gallery has been erected in the church, and both under and over it, are many neat memorials of strangers, mostly in younger life, who have here finished their mortal course; a few of them are here transcribed as specimens of the whole.

A square marble slab thus preserves the memory of a West Indian physician:
Near this plaee Ke the remains of
Nathaniel Marchant, Esq.
a native of the Island of Antigua,
Where his abilities as a physician, a magistrate, and a legislator, and the many amiable qualities of his mind, will be held in admiration while memory shall last. He died the 25th of February, 1804, in the 49th year of his age, and his disconsolate widow, after receiving uninterrupted proofs of his affection for 18 years, caused this stone to be erected to his memory.
Four black and white marbles, of very neat workmanship, occur in succession, and are inscribed as follow:
Near this spot are deposited the remains of

Charles Watson, Esq.
of Saughton, in the county of Mid. Lothian, who died here, June 2, 1804, aged 66.
"In te, Domine, speravi."
The second has the arms of the deceased at the top, the motto, "Deo Non Fortuna."
Inside this Church, and underneath, lies the body of
William Henry Digby, Esq.
third and last remaining son of John W. Digby, Esq. of Lauderstown, C-Kildare, died at
Sidmouth, 10 Feb. A. D. 1809, aged 22 years.
The third, is thus inscribed,
Underneath are deposited the remains of
Catharine, wife of George Stacpoole, Esq.
of Grosvenor Place, in the County of Middlesex, who departed this life, October 28,1809, *Mtat.* 37.
The fourth, which is surmounted by a figure of Hope, is thus worded,
O Lord receive my soul.
Close to, and underneath this stone are deposited the remains of
Charlotte Temperance, eldest surviving daughter of
Thomas and Elizabeth Alston, of Odell Castle, Bedfordshire.
She died at Sidmouth, on the 10th of November, 1810, aged nineteen.

One of the most recent, as well as appropriate of these mural records, is in the form of a Sarcophagus, and placed near the communion table; it is thus inscribed:
In a vault are deposited the remains of Maria Elizabeth, second daughter, and «o-heiress of the late Thomas Dyot Bucknall, Esq. of Hampton Court, in the County of Middlesex, who came to Sidmouth for the benefit of her health, and, after a Jong illness, borne with pious resignation, and in the exercise of every social virtue, departed this life, to the inexpressible grief of ker family, April 16, 1814, aged 26.
Early, bright, transient, chaste as morning dew,
She sparkled, was exhaled, and sent to heaven.

In the *church-yard,* as Sidmouth becomes more cele brated for the winter as well as the summer retreats of invalids, every year adds to the number of tomb-stones. Many of them, as may easily be supposed, are erected over the remains of those, who, seeking too late the renovating breezes of this charming place, have here paid the debt of nature. Several of these mortuary erections are in a handsome, substantial style. One of them records the name of the Reverend Samuel Black all, B. D. rector of Loughborough, who was so delighted with Sidmouth, while living, as to wish to be buried in this church-yard. He was the grandson of Dr. Offspring Blackall, who was bishop of Exeter in the reign of Queen Anne, and, from the great interest which her mat jesty took in his elevation, denominated the queen's bishop.

A handsome tomb, near the belfry door, thus records some branches of the Cotmaton family:

On one side,

In memory of Henry Carslake, gent. of Cottinton, in this parish, who died the 17th day of July, 1757, in the 59th year of his age: Also, Elizabeth, his wife, who died the 20th day of June, 1744, in the 35th year of her age: Also, Joseph Carslake, their son, who died August the 6th, 1757, in the 18th year of his age: Also, Anna Maria, their daughter, who died an infant.

On the opposite side, M

Henry Carslake, of Cottinton, gent. died January 20th, 1760, aetat. 29.

Lately, like you, I flourished in the fair field of life: in a moment the unexpected storm arose, which cut me down like a flower, and my body lies withering in this comfortless bed. Estimate from hence the value of earthly tilings: remember judgment, and learn to die.

Several of the newest tomb-stones are marked with a *cross,* an indication that the persons they commemorate, were Roman Catholics.

Enclosed by ad iron railing, on the south side of the church, the following testimony to the worth of an amiable lady occurs:

Here lieth the remains of Charlotte, wife of John StOrer, A. M. Rector of Hawkesworth, Notts; second daughter of Charles Wylde, D. D. Rector of St. Nicholas, Nottingham,

She was a rare gift of God, soon taken away; rich in the faith of a crucified Saviour, and that faith evidenced by its fruits a hdfy life. A flower eariy ripened by the eternal Spirit for immortal bliss; she left this present scene to her own joy, but to the sorrow of her surviving relatives, the 29th of January, 1816, aged 25, leaving three sons, John, Charles, and George.

The church of Sidmouth was granted in 1212, by '"Uisbop Marshall, to the monastery of *St. Michael de Monte,* in Normandy, to which the priory of Otterton was a cell. Sidmouth is now a *vicarage,* the rectorial tythes belong to Wadham-college, Oxford; and, for the vicarial, the inhabitants pay a composition. The Reverend William Jenkins, father of Thomas Jenkins, Esq. the lord of the manor, is the present incumbent. The vicarage-house is situated near the entrance of the town from the north. It is an old building modernized, and very considerably enlarged and improved.

A House near the beach, for many years known by the sign of the Anchor, afterwards a private dwelling, and about the year 1805 pulled down, is said to have been a *chapel of ease,* while Otterton was the motherchurch. The thickness of its stone walls, the firmness of the cement by which the stones were united, and its chapel-looking door-way arched with stone, certainly favoured this idea. In further confirmation of it, there ran near it a path leading from Sidbury and Sidmouth to Otterton, called *Go-church,* in which, till about twenty-five or thirty years ago, an ancient stone cross was standing: its situation, and the space it occupied, are still discoverable, by a difference in the pavement near the present market-house, THE OLD DISSENTING CHAPEL

Is situated at the north entrance of the town, at the corner of *Mill Lane.* It is a small, white, thatched building, measuring forty-five feet long and twenty-three broad. Its exterior appearance is very humble, but within, it is neat and con-

venient. It was erected between eighty and ninety years ago. Previous to that time, there was a meeting-house in what is now termed Theatre Lane.

It is uncertain at what time a regular dissenting congregation was formed in this place: most likely it was in the reign of Charles II. Mr. William Paulk is the first of their ministers, whose name has been preserved. He appears, as the minister of Sidmouth, to have delivered a sermon before the *assembly* at Exeter, September 9,1719.

The present minister is Mr. Edmund Butcher, who, having quitted London, onaccount of indisposition, in the year 1797, received so much benefit from residing in Devonshire, as to enable him, the following year, to accept a *unanimous invitation* to the pastorship of this society. Since then he has laid before the public two volumes of Sermons for the use of families, an Excursion from Sidmouth to Chester, and some other pieces.

In the month of June, 1811, an addition was made to the religious edifices of this town, by the opening of a very neat and commodious chapel, for the use of Protestant Dissenters of the Calvinistic persuasion. Its dimensions are about 30 feet by 40. It was erected by subscription, and has'one of those useful institutions, a *Sunday School,* supported by its attendants. The Rev. Mr. Ward is its present minister.

By the zeal and philanthrophy of some pious and public-spirited individuals, in the month of September, 1814, a Branch Bible Society, connected with the AuxIliary Bible Society at Exeter, was established at jSidmouth: the meeting upon the occasion was numerously attended. Lord Teignmouth, to whom this noble and truly Christian Institution is so deeply indebted, was kind enough to take the chair, and to accept, as was unanimously wished, the patronage of the Society.

A respectable list of subscribers was procured, and, on the first anniversary of the Institution, the following list of officers was presented to the public:

Patron,

Bight Honourable Lord Teignmouth.

President,
Sir John Kennaway, Bart.
Vice-Presidents,
George Cornish, Esq. Robert Hunt, Esq.
Treasurer,
Daniel Mackinnon, Esq.
Secretaries,
H. Van Hagen, Esq. Mr. M. Hall.

The Report made upon this occasion was a very satisfactory one, it concluded with the following animated paragraph:

"The times we live in are in every respect extraordinary; but novel and unprecedented as the occurrences in the political world are, they are surpassed in interest and importance by the scenes which are now exhibiting, in the endeavours for the moral and religious amelioration of mankind; and while political events are shrouded in obscurity, and we hardly know the final result of any of the transactions we witness, we know assuredly, that the spread of the Scriptures shall terminate in the realization of that glorious day, when the kingdoms of this world shall become the kingdoms of our Lord and of his Christ, and he shall reign for ever and ever. In hope of the fulfilment of these predictions, we are encouraged to persevere in our exertions; and are assured by Him who cannot lie, that our labour shall not be in vain in the Lord. For ' His name (who is the sum and substance of the Bible) shall endure for ever; His name shall be continued as long as the sun, and men shall be blessed in Him; all nations shall call Him blessed, and blessed be His glorious name for ever, and let the whole" earth be filled with His glory. Amen, and Amen.'"

A very useful association has lately been formed for the double purpose of relieving real distress, and guarding the benevolent from imposition. It is denominated.

The Humane, Or Poor's Friend Society,
instituted in Sidmouth, December 15,1815,
for the purpose of-visiting and relieving the sick and distressed poor of Sidmouth, and its vicinity, at their own

Habitations.

Mr. William Robins is the Treasurer, and
Mr. Matthew Hall, the Secretary.

The following passages, from the address circulated upon the subject, will further explain the nature of its design, and the progress it has actually made:

"Visitors cannot relieve previous to the case being laid before the committee, unless they should deem it quite necessary to grant immediate assistance, when one shilling may be advanced, but not more.

"Subscribers to the Society are at liberty to recommend any case of distress, which may come to their knowledge, when visitors will, as quickly as possible, attend to such cases as shall be so recommended, and institute an enquiry into the name—parish—occupation — cause of distress—if married—number of children, with the ages of each—if application has been made to the parish, and amount of relief therefrom—relief or income from other sources, &c. 8cc.

"Visitors will avail themselves of every opportunity to check neglect and disorder in the families of the poor; and advise them on those necessary points of economy, in which they are often defective.

"-Many families and individuals have been found by this Society so completely stripped of their apparel, as to be unable, after the return of health, to gain any employment, for want of a decent appearance; and the funds of this Society not being adequate to the purchase of even *he* coarsest cloathing, they beg leave to solicit, from the friends and patrons of this Society, donations of cast-off or useless clothes, or any other cheap article of wearing apparel, suitable either for men or women, boys or girls; also blankets, sheets, &c. will be thankfully received, and appropriated with the greatest care to the most necessitous and prudent of the poor, by being sent to Mr. William Harris, grocer, Sidmoulh.

"*April 2d,* 1816. "K5" Since the formation of the before-mentioned Society, in December last, every exertion has been made by the visitors to find out

deserving objects of the charity, in Sidmouth and its vicinity. Relief has been afforded to sixty-four families and individuals, and not less than two hundred and sixty distinct visits made; particulars of which are entered in a register, deposited with the Secretary of the Society, and open at all times to the inspection of its friends and supporters. In administering and apportioning their relief, the committee have always attended to the circumstances of the persons requiring it, and have sometimes supplied them with articles of which they were in the more immediate want; and have adverted also to the parochial allowances, if any, which they have received."

This charity will hereafter be conducted under the superintendance of the under-mentioned magistrates and gentlemen of Sidmouth and its vicinity, some of whom will meet the Committee of the Society the third Monday of every month, at *one* o'clock, at the London Inn, Sidmouth, to co-operate, and give them all the assistance in their power.

Sir John Kennaway, Bart. Rev. Mr. Cockburn.
Sir Robert Wilmot, Bart. Rev. James-JJernard.
George Cornish, Esq. J. James, Esq.
Edward Lee, Esq. Smith Wright, Esq.
Daniel Mackinnon, Esq. J. C. Girardot, Esq.
Rev. H. Fellowes, Sidbury. Rev. Edmund Butcher.

One of those useful institutions A Savings Bank, having been established at Exeter, the Rev. Mr. CockBurn, and H. Cutler, Esq. have kindly undertaken to act as receivers at Sidmouth.

ACCOMMODATIONS, AMUSEMENTS, &c. There are three Inns in the town,—the London, the New Inn, and the York Hotel. The assembly and card rooms are at the London Inn; the assemblyroom is large and well fitted up, and generally well attended. The rooms are open for *cards* every night, and, during the season, there is a *ball* every Wednesday. Large parties are here frequently assembled; but no *master of the ceremonies* has hitherto been appointed. The want of such an officer is often sensibly felt, and especially by such of the visitants as have no previous acquaintance with any of the stated frequenters of the rooms.

For the few last seasons, the company have spent a great part of their evenings at the libraries.—It may well bear a question whether the *older,* and certainly more *sociable* mode upon the whole, of assembling at the rooms, is not a preferable way of passing the evening; nothing, however, is so valuable as fashion, or so completely under the dominion of caprice, as any particular mode of "killing time." That taste for music which is so much the characteristic of the present day, was, during the last winter, gratified at Sidmouth, by a number of both public and private concerts. A very respectable band is in its infancy, established by some tradesmen of the town, who in fine weather amuse the company with martial and other pieces—it is supported by voluntary subscription, which is received at Mr. Wallis's Library.

The York Hotel is a large handsome house, newly erected. It stands on the beach, and has an uninterrupted view of the whole bay in which Sidmouth Ties.

The London Inn bas a fine set of stables newly built, nearly opposite itself. The stables belonging-to the Hotel are higher up in the town, and are the same which formerly belonged to the London Inn.

The New Inn, is upon a smaller scale than either the London or the Hotel. Very good accommodations are to be met with here also, and it possesses a convenient stable. At the London Inn, and York Hotel, postchaises, good horses, and careful drivers are to be had.

Wines, porters, and liquors of all sorts are to be had, not only at the inns,. public-houses, and several shops in the town, but of the importer, Mrs. TremIie. tt, nearly opposite the Post-office.

Two breweries,—one carried on by Mr. Searle, in the northern suburb of the town, called *Land,* and the other by Mr. Baker, in the *Marsh,* supply the town and the visitors with a very excellent table beverage.

Broadbridge's Boarding-house in the Marketplace, no longer exists, but such an establishment is much wanted.

The Market-house is a convenient, modern brick edifice, surmounted with a ball and weathercock.

PROVISIONS

Are plentiful, and, in general, very good of their kinds. Beef, mutton, and pork, are excellent; and veal, though not so large, nor, by excessive bleeding, rendered so white as that brought to the London markets, is very sweet. Saturdays and Tuesdays are the chief market days, but several butchers reside in the town, and every day the supply is commonly equal to the demand. Poultry and eggs, are brqught by the country-people to the doors of the in habitants: the poultry is both good and cheap. Bread and cakes are supplied in abundance by several bakers. Vegetables and fruit are furnished by the gardeners of the place: of these Arnoll, Barret, and Franklin are, at this time, the principal. Fruit is also brought in from the neighbouring parishes, even from Taunton, and other distant places.

LODGINGS

Are numerous, and may be had of almost all sizes and prices, as well as in a variety of situations. They are scattered in every part of the town and its vicinity. Those on the beach, and in the Fortfield, possessing an unbroken view of the sea, are generally the most sought after. In the town, however, as more sheltered, invalids are often ordered to reside; and one great advantage of Sidmouth is, that almost every want of this sort may be supplied. Situations, open or sheltered, in the sunshine or the shade, public or private, may be obtained.

THE BEACH

Is the grand public mall: it is a delightful broad walk, upon the margin of the sea, railed and rolled in a very good style. It is nearly a third of a mile in length, and is furnished at the extremities, and in some other parts, with neatly painted, convenient double seats, from which either the land or the sea may be contemplated with every advantage.

Adjoining Mr. Hodges' "Medical Baths," which are nearly in the middle of the Beach, is a large handsome billiard-room, in which there is an excellent table, and every suitable accommodation. Going westward, towards the Fort, is WALLIS'S MARINE LIBRARY; established June 20, 1809, under the immediate patronage of Lord Gwydir, Lady Willoughby, Lord and LadyLeDespenser, Emmanuel BaruhLousada, Esq. and the principal nobility and gentry of the town and neighbourhood. This establishment first furnished to Sidmouth what it had long wanted, a Iounging-place in a conspicuous and pleasant situation, where articles of fancy, as well as information and utility, may be met with; where the news of the day may be collected and discussed, and an opportunity given to the saunterers at a watering place to chat and gossip together. No situation can be more favourable for all these purposes than the Marine Library. It commands, from its delightful *Veranda,* a near and utterly unimpeded view of the sea. Large parties are often chatting on its benches: the gay and healthy are amused, and the invalid finds a spot from which he can inhale those salubrious breezes which so frequently suspend the ravages of disease, pour fresh oil into the lamp of life, and send him back, with renovated energies, to both the cares and the joys of mortality.

The Library opens directly upon that charming *promenade* the *Beach,* where all the beauty and fashion of the place are often collected. It is well supplied *every day* with the London and provincial newspapers. Several of the most popular periodical publications are to be found upon its tables. A variety of elegant toys and trinkets, and some articles of greater utility, occupy its shelves. Books of education, dissected maps, and a circulating library, to which *new* works are regularly added, complete an establishment which, with the liberal encouragement so long experienced, will be, every season, increasing in variety and value. A part of the shop in which, when necessary, a good fire is always kept, is appropriated to the readers of the newspapers and other periodical publications.

Another Library has since been opened by Mr. Marsh, towards the east end of the beaoh. It is a large, handsome room, with a colonnade in front, and commanding a full view of the sea, but the elegant *rural* scenery which is to be seen from the original establishment is wanting.

A most beautiful and faithful *panoramic* view of the whole beach, including all the buildings upon it, the rocks at each extremity, and the hills in the back ground, has been drawn by Hubert Cornish, Esq. engraved in aqua tinta by Havell, and published by Wallis, opposite whose library the view was taken.

It may be mentioned as a proof of the distance at which objects may be seen from the beach, as well as a memorable historical fact, that from the veranda of the Marine Library, the Right Hon. Lord Gwydir and Lord Charles Bentinck witnessed the entrance into Torbay of his Majesty's ship Bellerophon, with Napoleon Bonaparte on board.

The lodging-houses upon the beach, and near it, having a view of the sea, are about *forty,* terminating with Bock Cottage, at the west end, belonging to Mr. Joseph Sparks, and commanding a view of the whole beach, and the eastern cliffs. Immediately beyond Rock Cottage, and crowning a projecting rock, is a small thatched cottage, built by E. B. Lousada, Esq. To this division of habitations, which, from its detached and elevated situation, might be denominated *Clifton,* Mr. Heffer has added a new house, which *D* overlooks the lower end of the Ham, in which King'3 Cottage is situated.

Except the billiard, card, and assembly rooms, Sidmouth has no place of public amusement. Some years ago, a small theatre was erected: an itinerant company were the performers; but the building, now converted into dwelling-houses, is a proof of the success they met with. This, however, has not prevented another attempt. A substantial building near the beach has been fitted up for the purpose; the scenery and performers were both above mediocrity, and the only season in which they have

performed, which was in the autumn of 1814, they were respectably attended.
EDUCATION.
For this important purpose a provision is here made.

Miss Bryett keeps a most respectable boarding and day school for young ladies.

Mr. Edward Evans has carried on a day school for many years.

His daughter, Miss Evans, keeps a day school for young ladies.

The French language is taught, at the houses of the pupils, by Mons. Thebaut.
THE ENVIRONS OF SIDMOUTH.
By these are meant the houses and estates scattered in the immediate vicinity of the town, which adorn, not merely the flat part of the vale, but the slopes of the hills which bound'it on either side. In the flat part of the valley, west of the town, and open to the sea, a row of brick houses appear, in number eleven, which, if finished according to the plan laid down, would form a crescent with a small curve. These, with the exception of No. 6, belonging to Mrs. Fulford, are all let for hire, and for any time agreed upon. The field in which they stand is called the *Fort Field,* from a little fort at the end of it, in which there are still four old pieces of cannon, but the flag-staff and small ammunition-house have long ago disappeared.

Entering the Fort Field from Wallis's Library, the first buildings that offer themselves are *two* convenient and roomy houses, built by Mr. Denby—the view from them, both of Peak Hill, and the sea to the westward is very beautiful.
Fort House, built by Mr. Philips, and since become the property of Sir John Kennaway, Bart. by whom it has been greatly enlarged and beautified, stands on the *eastern* side of the Fort Field: it is a large house, very tastefully furnished, and is now occupied by A. Dashwood, Esq.
Close by it, is *Barton Cottage,* a neat and convenient residence, built by the late Mr. Follett. Immediately adjoining, is a *large house,* well fitted up, and built for the purpose of letting, by Mr. Rafarel, pastry-cook and confectioner.

Close by the entrance into the Fort Field, opposite the church, is a small house and garden, belonging to Miss Pleydell.

Going up the Fort Field, from Mr. Rafarel's, and separated from it by a lane, stands *Rosemount,* a very pleasant habitation, erected by C. E. Pigou, Esq. and at a little distance another, of nearly the same size, denominated *High Bank.*
D2
At the northern end of tie Fort Field, about a quarter of a mile from the church, is *Cottington,* or *Cotmaton,* " an ancient seat, commanding a pleasant view of the bay. It was sold by the Dukes of Otterton, to William. Harlewin, Esq. Sir John Harlewin, who was knighted for his valour in the time of Edward IV. lived at Sidmouth. His descendants lived at Sidmouth to the time of Charles II. Cotmaton is now the property of Mrs. Elizabeth Carslake, whose brother, the late John Carslake, Esq. in the year 1809, removed into *New Cotmaton,* a house which he built, almost adjoining the old one. Its front looks full on the sea, and, like the terrace, in its beautiful garden, commands a fine view of it.

Witheby, the elegant cottage, planned and built by Miss Floyd, stands at the head of a fine verdant meadow, which slopes down to the Fort Field, with which it is connected by a neat little bridge. This beautiful *cottage ornee* has been enlarged and decorated by the taste and spirit of its present possessor, Miss Wrighte, in such a manner, as to render it a most lovely residence. The new carriage approach from Mill Lane, while it increases the convenience of access, adds a new beauty to the scenery around it.

On the right hand, approaching Miss Wrighte's, with a beautiful lawn and shrubbery before it, and an excellent walled garden, rises the well designed and highly finished house of the Reverend James Hobson: the view from the lawn, both of sea and land, is rich and extensive. The lodge belonging to this mansion, which stands opposite the entrance into the grounds in Mill Lane, is an object of universal admiration. The ivy which creeps up its slender pillars, and hangs in festoons from *its* roof, gives it a simple elegance which no other ornament could have bestowed.

Just at the entrance of the town, at the corner of Mill Lane, stands a substantial brick house, formerly the best in Sidmouth, and long the only one of the kind. It was for many years the residence of the late Mr. Oxenham, and now adds one to the lodging-houses of the place. Going from thence towards Exeter, we come to the *Vicarage,* and a little further on, to *Bolsters,* now the residence of Samuel Giles, Esq. The principal houses in the town are Myrtle Hall, the residence of Henry Manning, Esq. That built by General Grinfield, now the property and residence of H. Cutler, Esq. and the Rev. Mr. Le Merchant's.

Ascending Mill Lane from Mr. Oxenham's, on the left hand, is *Rose* Cottage, now the residence of Mrs. Bird. It was built by Mr. William Stocker, to whom also belongs a small neat cottage nearly opposite.

Further up Mill Lane, and at the corner of Church Lane, is the *Rustic* Cottage of Lord Gwydir, which, when the family are absent, is permitted to be seen by strangers. The exterior of this house, which was altered by his lordship from a farm house called *Old Hayes,* has a fanciful and unique appearance. Its garden, which is but small, is partly an orchard: on the whole northern side of it runs a covered walk of uncommon simplicity and beauty. The roof, the interior of which is formed of straight sticks, with the bark left on, is supported by two rows of oaken pollards, round which roses, honey-suckles, the clematis, and other climbing shrubs and flowers, twine themselves. The walk is terminated by a small room, with seats, framed of the same rustic materials, which has the appearance of a hermitage, or chapel: the whole has very much the air of the cloister of some religious edifice.

Adjoining to Lord Gwydir's is *Spring Gardens,* the residence of W. D. Fellowes, Esq. Immediately beyond this, Major Sandford, of the Somersetshire Militia, is now erecting a house; and in the field opposite Lord Gwydir's, a most desirable spot for such a purpose, Miss Floyd, it is hoped, will once more display her architectural taste.

On a beautiful eminence, to the north of Major Sandford's, a few years ago, Lord Le Despenser erected a *Marine Villa*—it is a large thatched building, forming nearly a quadrangle. It contains about forty rooms, many of which are large, and fitted up in a style of simple elegance. His Lordship sold this fanciful mansion before it was completed. Being offered as a lodging-house, it was hired by the late Marquis of Bute. The view from it is extremely rich and picturesque.

Still ascending Mill Lane, on the right hand, opposite Cotmaton, is the residence of the Reverend James Bernard. This gentleman has shewn great taste, both in the internal and external alterations, by which he has converted a mean looking brick house into one of the most interesting cottages in the vicinity of Sidmouth. The judicious manner in which he has *thinned* the luxuriant trees and shrubs with which he found the grounds crowded, while it enlarges his prospect, has really increased the beauty of the scene. Trees are, no doubt, a great beauty in a landscape, but it is possible to have too many of them.

Passing some small cottages, Miss Mills's *pretty* bouse, and Mr. Hobson's Lodge, we find, nearly opposite Miss Wrighte's carriage-way and shrubbery, *Helens,* a house belonging to the Reverend Edmund Butcher, now in the possession of Sir George Armytage, Bart, and next to it the handsome mansion of Edward Lee, Esq. Very considerable additions are making to it, and the shrubs and trees in its front, and on its wings, are, every year, increasing its beauty. Both these houses are delightfully situated, and between the trees, which flourish luxuriantly about them, have charming views of the sea and the surrounding country.

Proceeding towards the hill, the extremely neat lodge of *Peak House,* the property and residence of the hospitable Emanuel Barub Lousada, Esq. is the next object of attention. The drive from the lodge up to the house is uncommonly fine—on the *right* hand a shrubbery full of fragrance and beauty, through the greater part of which there is a serpentine foot-path, and on the *left,* an unbroken view of the ocean, at all times an interesting and elevating spectacle. The mansion itself, which has been built by that gentleman, with its grounds and gardens, in which still further improvements are projected, is a delightful abode. It is a considerably elevated situation, and commands a fine reach of the ocean, the white and yellow cliffs of Bere, Charmouth, and Bridport, and the bold promontory of Portland.

Considerably above Mr. Baruh's, erected by him, and standing on his estate, are two small houses; one is a fanciful building, which, before its battlements were removed, had something of the appearance of a small fort. The other, which has a veranda, has a stable and coachhouse attached to it. It is needless to add, what a noble, diversified, and extensive view is to be had from the windows of each of these mountain houses.

On the southern extremity of Peak Hill stands a *signal house,* now happily untenanted. In fine weather this is often the boundary of a ride or a walk, and the lovers of landscape beauty, not only from this point, but in the several stages of their progress, are richly rewarded for the labour of the ascent, by the vast *pariorama* which spreads its ample circle around them. Sea and land unite in this picture: if any vessels are passing;, here they must be visible; and on the land side the prospect is replete with all the charms which nature and art can give to such a scene. The ridges of the hills, which, in every direction, bound the view, are for the most part without cultivation; but this comparative sterility only serves to augment the richness of the general prospect: by the contrast, the fine foliage of the trees and hedges is shown. to the greater advantage. Fertility and beauty unite in every part of the scene— the landscape is complete, the earth clothed with verdure, the air balmy and refreshing, orchards and gardens, hills of all dimensions, large stacks of hay and corn, and a multitude of habitations, many of them a pure white, which harmonizes so well with the azure above and the green below. The tops of the hills afford full scope for the entertainment and health which are combined in *equestrian* exercise.

At the *western* extremity of the Fort Field, is *Belmont,* the property of Sir Joseph Scott, Bart, who has made very considerable additions and improvements, both in the house and grounds, since it came into his possession. In a narrow low slip of ground, called a *ham,* immediately adjoining, which is watered by a serpentine stream, and by nature forming a lovely dell, is a pretty white habitation, called, from the gentleman who built it, *King's Cottage.*

Close by the church-yard, commanding a beautiful view into the country, and looking upon a pleasant meadow, is Amyat's Place, a row of small houses, built in an uniform manner by the late J. Ararat, Esq. in one of which is kept one of Dr. Bell's schools, where are educated about forty children. Going up tho lane, immediately above Sir John Kennaway's stables, *two* small lodging-houses form one side of a square, the higher end of which is occupied by a neat house, termed, from the year in which it was erected, *Jubilee* Cottage.

On the left hand of the lane, beyond Rafarel's stables, stands an old house, with a garden and summer-house, which looks into the Fort Field, and has a fine view of Peak Hill. The *rope-zcalk,* running through an orchard, succeeds, in the same lane—it runs behind Rosemount, just beyond which is a small neat box, which bears the name of *Elmtree* Cottage.

The house built by the Rev. P. Story is a plain, handsome building, in one of the most secluded situations in Sidmouth; it stands in a pleasant garden, between what may be called the High Street and the church, and from its upper windows has a fine western view. It has a carriage-way from the street, and a footway into the small, sheltered fields known by the name of *Blackmoor.*

On the eastern side of Sidmouth Valley, after passingdown the marsh, and leaving, on the left hand, Mr. Baker's brewery, the poor-house, and, further on, the water-mill, and a neat house, newly erected, the river presents itself, across which a neat wooden bridge conveys the passenger into Saloombe parish. Directly opposite the bridge is the foot-path to *Salcombe Hill,* the mansion of George Cornish, Esq. This edifice, which has a handsome colonnade in front, and the luxuriant and beautiful scenery with which it is surrounded, enrich and adorn the eastern boundary of Sidmouth.

Myrtle Cottage, decorated by the taste of Miss Campbell, is delightfully situated, immediately under Salcombe Hill; the exterior of its beautiful garden is washed by the Sid; its present possessor, A. J. Ram, Esq. is enlarging the house, and adding to its attractive scenery. *Egypt,* a small house belonging to G. Cornish, Esq. is pleasantly perched, like a nest in a grove, upon the lowest ridge of Salcombe Hill, directly above Myrtle Cottage. From Mr. Cornish's grounds, which extend to the sea, a near view of the town is to be obtained— the little bay in which it is secluded—many of the indentations of the coast—the deep-ribbed side of the High Peak, the western boundary of the ever-memorable *Torbay,* and *Berry Head,* which appears plunging into the distant waves, and marking the line which separates the sky from the land. It is thought that the most extensive land view is to be had from this *eastern* height; the eye ranges over a space of at *hast forty* miles, and rests the extremity of its vision upon the most elevated points of *Dartmoor.*

The public road towards Lyme passes in front of a lodging-house called *Mount Pleasant;* and up rather a steep ascent, on the *right* hand, as it enters *Sid,* or *Seed* Lane, presents the passenger with a glimpse of *Salcombe Cottage,* the property and residence of C. Sedgwick, Esq.

On the *left* hand, in Sid Lane, delightfully situated in a fine lawn, and surrounded with sylvan scenery, is *Salcombe House,* the property, and, for a part of the year, the residence of the Rev. Mr. Cockburn: the river, which runs through the grounds, and on the side of which there is a walk open to the. public, is, especially when swollen by rain, a fine feature in the landscape.

A little beyond Salcombe House is *Hill's Cottage,* built by Mrs. Leigh, of Slade, and now occupied by J. James, Esq. On the right hand of the lane, beyond Hill's Cottage, is the new house of Thomas Lyde, Esq. and in a field nearly opposite, the elegant box of R. Miles, Esq. At a still greater distance from the town, lies *Sid Cliff,* once the secluded and truly romantic cottage of Edmund Boehm, Esq. now the property of Captain Clark, who has converted the late stables, which, in the opinion of many people, were much more pleasantly situated than the house, into a very desirable residence for himself.

For the indulgence of that occasional retirement from the world which is so conducive to health of body, and to the refreshment and vigour of the mind, and in which wise and virtuous spirits have, at all times, so much delighted, the immediate vicinity of Sidmouth is peculiarly calculated:—it abounds with lanes, many of them of considerable length and variety, more or less sequestered, and at all times perfectly safe, in which, either on foot or horseback, the delights of solitude, or of society upon a small scale, may be enjoyed. The *beach,* on the contrary, offers to such as are most happy in a crowd, whose grand enjoyment it is to see and be seen, a walk, in which, at almost all times, amusement and health are to be found. Few, indeed, are those days in the year, on which, in some part or other of them, if not the whole, a promenade on the beach is not dry and agreeable.

After a storm, considerable quantities of *marine plants,* which have been torn from the beds upon which they grow, are left upon the sand and pebbles below the beach:—as the drying and preserving of these is, to many, a very interesting amusement, the following directions, taken from 'Donovan's Instructions for collecting and preserving Subjects of Natural History,' are submitted to their notice.

All the smaller plants should be expanded under water, in a plate, upon a piece of writing-paper, sunk to the bottom. In this state they will assume their natural form and position. The paper, with the plant upon it, must be withdrawn from the water gently; and the plant and paper must' afterwards be placed between two or three sheets of blotting-paper, and pressed with a book or flat board. When taken from hence, it is to be put between fresh sheets of paper, Until all the moisture appears to be gone. It is then to be laid up in a quire of blotting-paper, under pressure for a day or two, when, if *dry,* it may be placed permanently upon writing-paper. The larger coriaceous kinds require a good deal of drying, in successive changes of paper, and in a very dry room, or near the fire. When once dried, and put into a herbarium, they seldom become damp again.

BATHING,

That salutary and pleasant custom, that chief avowed reason for which such numbers every year quit the towns, and crowd to the coast of our island, and so important an article to the invalid, is, at Sidmouth, both commodious and reasonable. Eight machines, which are conveniently pfaced a little to the westward of the town, are constantly ready: the terms are, *one shilling* for each gentleman the *first* time, and *sixpence* for every time afterwards. Ladies one shilling and sixpence the first time, and one shilling after.

WARM SEA BATHS

Fitted up in an extremely convenient and comfortable manner, have been established, both by Mr. Hodge and Mr. Stocker; they embrace every mode of bathing.

To assist these means of preserving and restoring health, besides a physician, Dr. James Clarke, five or six surgeons and apothecaries constantly reside in Sidmouth.

Those persons who are fond of swimming, or prefer bathing without the use of a machine, should be informed, that a little to the west of the beach there is a fine sequestered bay, in which they

may, in calm weather, be safely gratified. The border is a fine sand; upon which, at high water, the bather may walk for a long distance *out,* without being immersed higher than the breast.

"Sea.bathing," says Dr. Buchan, "is good for one reason, because the sea is a *cold bath.* The time of bathing ought to be postponed till past noon, or at least till some hours after breakfast, when the digestion of that meal may be supposed to be terminated; and such a degree of exercise should always be taken previously to entering the water, as may be sufficient to produce a sensation of warmth over the whole body. By no means go into the water chilly." CLIMATE.

Theair of Sidmouth is sometimes moist, but always pure, and, with very few exceptions, mild and soft. There are no stagnant waters in its vicinity, but, as has been already remarked, a number of the purest streams constantly flowing.

Many of the faculty think the air of Sidmouth equal to that of the south of France, and very commonly recommend it to invalids, particularly to those who are affected by, or have a tendency to consumptions. The natives and stated inhabitants of the place are, in general, healthy and strong, and live to a good old age. *Eighty* and *ninety* are ages frequently to be met with, and some few live to more than a *hundred* years.

A striking proof of the mildness of the Sidmoutb air is, that both the large and small leaved myrtles are planted out of doors, and bear the winter without any shelter: against many houses and garden walls they rise to a great height. All kinds of geraniums, phusias, and other tender plants, nourish luxuriantly at this place, with a very little attention.

It is remarkable, that storms very seldom occur in this part of Devonshire: the thunder is generally very distant, and the lightning mild and beautiful; it is often seen when no thunder can be heard—a proof that the explosion takes place at a great distance. This general freedom of the south of Devonshire from storms is so established a fact, t that Mrs. Piozzi, who, in the year 1788, passed some time at Exmouth, thus em-

phatically refers to it, in a prologue which she wrote for a company of itinerant players, who were then performing at that place.

"By many a wave, by many a tempest tost,
Our shipwreck'd hopes we cast on Devon's coast,
Where the soft season swells the ripening grain,
And verdure brightens with refreshing rain;
Wliere lightnings never glare, nor thunders roar,
And chilling blasts forget their freezing power."

Occasional storms, however, are by no means to be considered as an unnecessary part of the economy of nature. "After, by a storm, the lower stratum of the atmosphere has been thoroughly mixed with the surface of the water of the sea, the air is more pure and salubrious. Even hurricanes improve the healthiness of the climates where they take place."—How just, as well as pious, upon this subject, is the remark of Dr. Buchan!

"Thus, while contemplating the tempest, that in its rage appears to convolve sea and sky, we learn to revere the Author of nature, who in his wisdom has ordained this awful instrument, which, while it sweeps from the surface of the earth that noxious vapour, whose accumulation would eventually put an end to animal existence, blends it with the agitated waters of the ocean, in whose bosom it becomes harmless, and is, probably, rendered subservient to some useful purpose."

Sometimes, at Sidmouth, as in other parts of England, a very hot day occurs, and then the following account, given by Dr. Maton, is accurate; but it is seldom that, even in such cases, the heat is not tempered by a refreshing breeze. "At the time of a clear summer sky, Sidmouth is intensely hot: its low situation, a broad bed of pebbles, and the glare of the lofty red cliffs, act as so many reverberators."

The West of England has been commonly considered as more rainy than almost any other part of the island. This is by no means a well-established fact. A gentleman, at Plymouth, not long ago, assured us, in one of the periodical publications, that, by comparing the accounts which he, and a friend of his in the upper part of Yorkshire, had kept for some years, of the quantity of rain which fell in those two distant points, the balance was in favour of the West; that is, during-that period more rain fell in Yorkshire than at Plymouth. In the vicinity of the sea, and in the neighbourhood of lofty hills, it may, perhaps, be admitted, that in general more rain falls than in an open level country.

A gentleman of Sidmouth has furnished this work with the following table of the number of days on which *any* rain has fallen at that place, since the 1st of *January* 1800. Perhaps on full half of them, only *one* shower, and that, frequently, an inconsiderable one, caused the day on which it fell to be put on the black list. In looking, therefore, at the number of wet days, this circumstance is to be recollected.

RAIN AT SIDMOUTH:
Years. Wef. Dry.
1800 146...219 1801 147 218 1802 147 218 1803 134 231 1804 162 203 1805 151 214 1806 178....187 1807 165 200 1808 178 187 1809 192.....173 1810 182 183 1811 185 180 1812 175 190 1813 147 218 1814 147 218 1815.170 195

In these sixteen years, therefore, the average number of wet days, as before described, appears to be 163, within *two. Lowest State of the Thermometer at the following plates, Friday Morning, February* 9, 1816.

Stamford Hall, Leicestershire, a little after) eight o'clock in the morning........ .. 3

Nottingham, half past seven 4 2

Exeter, by a Register 18 0

Heavitree, at eight 21 0

Sidmouth, by a Register, 21 0 NATURAL PRODUCTIONS.

Among the cliffs, and in the beautiful shady lanes of Sidmouth, the lover of natural history may find much to study, and much to amuse him. The botanist may cull a variety of plants, and the admirer *of fossils* collect many of the cu-

rious internal productions of the earth. *Pholens* of great beauty are occasionally met with, and the stones of the cliffs, many of them, are mixed with *echina marina,* petrified coral, and other similar productions. The *cornu ammotiis* is to be found here, of all sizes: one of the inhabitants of the town has got a very fine one, of an embellished metallic appearance, above twenty inches in diameter, which he found in the cliffs.

In the little basins, worn by the waves in the rocks, elegant corallines abound; and not unfrequently, that wonderful marine production the semone, or animal flower. It is difficult, indeed impossible, to decide to which of the kingdoms of nature, the animal or vegetable, this half-animated substance belongs. It possesses a kind of fungus consistency, by which it adheres to the rocks, while the part presented to the eye has the appearance of a multitude of small snakes, E of various and beautiful colours, which, diverging from a centre, spread into a circle, something like the corolla of the anemone, from which it derives its name—these threads are in constant motion. This creature is found in the little pools among the rocks, where it is constantly covered with water.

Spars, transparent and orystalized, in various forms, particularly the *rhomboidal* and *hexangular,* are found in various parts of Devonshire. On a great number of the lime rocks, calcareous incrustations are found. Lime and marble are produced in almost all parts of the country, except the moor-stone districts. Many of these marbles, as the chimney-pieces of most of the new houses of Sidmouth prove, for their hardness and beautiful veinings, rival the best Italian marble, and when polished, fall very little short of it in lustre. Most of the marble of Devonshire which is not black, is a sort of flesh colour, with brownish spots and veins of different shades. The late Lord Courtenay had specimens of all the different marbles in this county, in small squares, polished; and Lord Clifford has lately presented a large table, formed of similar materials, to the "Literary and Philosophical INSTITUTION" at Exeter. »

Very beautiful specimens of the' stones and fossils of this coast may be seen, and purchased, at LuxTON's, in the Market-place; and at Kingwill's Repository, near the Post Office, equally fine specimens of marble.

Some smaller collections are also to be met with.

THE LIME

Upon this coast is, in general, very plentiful, and some of it of a very good quality. It is used in great quantities for manure, as well as the usual purposes to which lime is applied. A lime-stone quarry was wrought some years ago, at Little Gatcombe, in the parish of Colyton. There are lime-quarries at Branscombe and Salcombe, which are worked in the following manner: The workmen cut a large opening near the sea, take off the head, wheel it to the cliff, and there discharge their loads into the sea, as the cliff is exceedingly high and steep. They have kilns upon the spot to burn the lime. The cliffs on each side of Torbay, Berryhead, Hope'snose, and so round to Babbacombe, are entirely of limestone.

Alabaster is found in great plenty in the cliffs near Sidmouth, as well as in various other parts of Devonshire; its texture is granular, with shining particles: it is a deposition from the water that distils through the lime-stone rocks.

As Geology, a branch of science so highly interesting in itself, is every day becoming more popular, the author of this work is happy in having it in his power to enrich it with the following geological remarks upon *South Devon,* from the pen of Mr. Robert Bakewell, Mineralogical Surveyor, the well-known author of the Introduction to Geology, &c.

"TO THE REV. E. BUTCHER.

"My dear Sir,

"In compliance with your request to communicate my observations on the geology of the country in the vicinity of Sidmouth, I send you the following brief remarks on some of the leading features, which may interest the general reader.

"The *southern* coast, from Portland Head to ExE2.

mouth, exhibits a fine section of the different *strata* as they rise in succession to the south-west, the sea having laid bare the surface, and presented a perpendicular face of rock nearly along the whole line. The southern counties, *east* of Portland, Hampshire, Sussex, and Kent, are almost exclusively occupied with rocks of the *chalk* formation, and their accompanying beds of sand and clay. The *roe-stone,* which succeeds. terminates at Portland. Between Portland and Bridport Bay there appears to have been a considerable break in the strata, and the *green sand,* which, in its regular position, is above the roe-stone, may be seen rising from the sea, *east of* Bridport: this stratum, which is provincially *caWed fox-mold,* extends far to the west, as we shall have subsequently to observe.

"The *blue lias,* covered by the green sand, rises from the sea nearBridport, and extends from thence to the river *Ax,* with little interruption. This is the most remarkable and best characterised of any of the British strata; the whole thickness of this bed cannot be less than *tioo hundred yards.* It is composed of numerous thin strata of dark grey limestone, combined with much clay and iron, and some manganese. Many of the strata form an excellent water limestone; the beds of dark clay which intervene abound with *pyrites,* and have been known to take fire spontaneously. The strata rises gradually to the south-west, but there are numerous faults, or breaks, which throw them down on the western side of such breaks from *ten* to *thirty* feet.

"Large masses from the perpendicular cliffs of Jias are constantly falling down, and discovering the imbedded petrifactions of numerous tribes of extinct animals. The lias limestone is the lowest of the British limestones that contain the remains of oviparous quadrupeds, or of any vertebrated animals, that is, such which have a brain and spinal marrow. Remains of fossil alligators, in a mutilated state, are very frequently found. I was fortunate enough to obtain part of a *small jaw,* very perfect; on comparing it with the

drawings of *Cuvier,* it nearly resembles that of the *Gangetic crocodile.* About a mile west of Lime, there is a small formation of chalk at Pinney, resting on the fox-mold, over the lias. The has continues to near Axminster, where several of the lower beds lose their dark grey eolour, and are called *white lias.* This white lias may be seen distinctly resting on the red marie *east* of Axminster.

"It may be proper to observe, that the same bed of lias runs *northward,* through Dorset, Somersetshire, and Gloucestershire, and into some of the *northern* counties of England, carrying with it, in its whole extent, numerous fossil remains of ammonites, pentacrinites, nautilites, scaly fish, and the bones of alligators. Near Bath, it is more indurated and crystaline than in Dorsetshire. The red marie, which succeeds the lias, is suddenly broken on the west side of the Ax, and a small formation of chalk makes its appearance at Beer, where we are presented with a fantastic range of chalkrocks and caverns, the chalk forming perpendicular cliffs, projecting into the sea. The *fox mold,* or green sand, succeeds, and then the red marie, which extends from near Beer to Sidmouth, and to the west of Exmouth, constituting a range of precipitous cliffs, rising from the sea more than 800 feet, in several parts of its course, particularly in Salcombe and Peak Hills. The *red marie,* as it has been denominated by some geologists, consists of silicious particles, mixed with clay, and deeply coloured by the red oxyd of iron: various beds of stratified sand-stone occur in it, particularly at Heavitree, near Exeter; these strata are evidently of mechanical formation, and contain imbedded fragments of slate, and amygdaloid, similar to the rocks on the 'vest of Exeter.

"Geologists have been perplexed, in attempting to class the *red marie* with the rocks in Werner's system, some supposing it to occupy the place of what he denominates the *old red sand-stone.* But without stopping to inquire what place it occupies in any geological system, I will briefly state what place it really occupies in Devonshire.

"I have before observed, that it rises from under the lias lime-stone; now where this lime-stone occurs it is always above the *coal* formation, but, in the *south* of Devon, the coal formation is entirely wanting, and also the mountain lime-stone under the coal, and the red marie supplies the place of both, extending from the river *Ax* to some miles west of the *Ex,* where it is found resting on coarse slate, provincially called *shillet.—* The *east* side of Exeter stands on the red marie, the *west* on the slate or shillet. Near the termination of red marie on the west, various rocks of *basaltic* formation, provincially called *dun-stone,* frequently occur between the slate and the red marie, and, in many parts, the rocks of dun-stone project through the red marie.

"The *dun-stone* differs much in its quality; in some parts it is a *sienite,* and passes into *green-stone,* or *trap,* in other parts it is more like what the Germans would call a compact *grey-wache;* sometimes it assumes all the appearance of real *lava,* containing numerous hollow cells, and presenting a dry and burnt aspect: in this state it cannot be distinguished from many *volcanic lavus.* Were I to hazard a conjecture respecting the formation of the red marie, I should say that it had been derived from the *debris,* or waste, of extensive *basaltic* rocks, of which the present rocks of dun-stone are only the remains, and it adds probability to this opinion, that the red marie on the east side of the dun-stone is always filled with fragments of the same kind of rock with that which is in its more immediate vicinity. For a knowledge of this fact, I am indebted to J. W. Johnson, Esq. *Surgeon,* Exeter. The red marie, in some parts, contains beds of gypsum, and I should not think it improbable that rock-salt or brinesprings may exist in some parts of Devon occupied by this extensive *stratum.* I now return to speak of the *green sand* or *fox-mold,* whicli, though a member of the chalk formation, and immediately subjacent to chalk, is carried not only over the lias, but over the red marie, and forms *caps* on many of the highest hills, from *Black Down,* on the east, to *Hal Down,* six miles west of Exeter: it contains numerous silicious masses conglomerated, in which a kind of *opaque hornstone* may be traced, passing into *flint*—the flint also may be traced passing into beautiful *calcedony,* and the calcedony again forming into *quartz crystals.* I am satisfied that the process is now going on, though we are at present unacquainted with the causes by which it is effected. Numerous *marine shells, ammonites,* &c. occur in the green sand, proving incontestibly, that the highest hills in this part of Devonshire were once buried under the waves of the ocean, of which we have also a further proof in the heaps of rounded pebbles and gravel on the high ground between Sidmouth and Exeter. It would be foreign to the purport of my letter to describe the rocks below the red marie and dun-stone, but I may just observe, that the slate round Dartmoor is remarkably twisted and bent, and contains in some parts beds of *transition-limestone;* it is succeeded by *granite,* which Salcombe stone, and though some of it has been erected six hundred years, it is very little, if at all, worn by the weather. The Bransconibe stone is not supposed to bear the weather so well; and the free-stone of Beer is of a much softer nature, and finer grit than that of Salcombe. When hewn out of the quarry, the free-stone of Beer cuts as soft asthe Bath stone, which it greatly resembles. forms the base and summit of Dartmoor, and extends from thence, with some interruption, to the Land's End in Cornwall.

"I am, my dear Sir,
"With much esteem,
"Your's very truly,
"ROB. BAKEWELL." "13, Tavistock Street, Bedford Square, May 16, 1816."

The following Sonnet, written upon a return to Sidmouth, will not unsuitably close the first part of this little work
Sidraouth! Hygeia's chosen seat?
Again receive me: let me greet
Thy ruddy cliffs, thy pebbly beach,
Thy broad majestic ocean reach,
And streams that murmur thro' thy green retreat.
Thy primrose banks, thy balmy skies,

Thy lofty trees which graceful rise,
Thy lanes and orchards, mountain-bound,
Thy fields with ceaseless verdure crown'd,
And every gem which Flora's hand supplies.
Sweet realm of peace, my chosen home,
To thee with joy again I come:
The lamp of life but dimly burns, But when my step to thee returns,
With brighten'd ray shoots up the ruddy flame,
And lights afresh the renovated frame.

SIDMOUTH SCENERY.

PART II.

Amongst the attractions of a watering-place, those which are contained in the country immediately about it, must always be reckoned as some of the most considerable. It will be the object of this part of the volume, to point out the principal *rides* which branch out from Sidmouth.

The vicinity of Sidmouth, as has been already observed, is peculiarly fitted for pleasant rambles, and short picturesque rides. There are also several places in its neighbourhood, which may serve as good objects for still longer excursions: of these it will be proper to give a somewhat detailed account.

Sidmouth is distant from Otterton three miles, from Salterton seven, from Exmouth ten, from Lympstone ten, from Topsham twelve, from Exeter fifteen, from St. Mary Ottery seven, from Harpford four, from Honiton nine, from Colyton nine, from Seaton ten, from Beer seven, from Branscombe five, from Salcombe two, from Axminster fifteen, and from Lyme sixteen.

RIDE FROM SIDMOUTH, EASTWARD.
SALCOMBE, or the *Salt Vale,* now called Salcombe Regis, is a small parish, east of-Sidmouth, between two and three miles broad from west to east, that is, from Sidmouth town to a place in Branscombe called Weston Mouth. The sea coast of it is thus described. "The cliff beyond Sidmouth is of a red stone, beyond which there is a narrow valley, at the upper end of which the church of Salcombe is situated. Beyond this val-

ley rises another hill, having a high steep cliff towards the sea, the lower part of which is of red stone, and the upper part of freestone. Dipping towards the sea, on Salcombe Head, there is a quarry where stones are dug, as they are likewise in a narrow vale, which runs up between Salcombe Head and Dunscombe, the next headland eastward. The stone here lies near the surface in some places. The eastern side of this hill seems to have been much worked, and there is little doubt that the Salcombe stone, of which so great a quantity was used in building the Cathedral of Exeter, was dug on the side of this hill; for there are very few quarries in any other part of the parish.

The principal sorts of free-stone found in Devonshire, are dug in the adjoining parishes of Salcombe, Branscombe, and Beer. That at Salcombe is a sandy grit, closely united, rather coarser than the Portland stone, and very hard. It works easily in the quarry. A proof how well it bears the weather, is to be seen at the Cathedral of Exeter, the outside of which is all built of

The principal village of this parish is *Seed,* a long straggling place, which has been already mentioned as lying by the river *Sid,* and containing Salcombe House, Hill's Cottage, Sid Cliff, and Sid Abbey. The road from Sidmouth to Lyme passes through it, and falls into the road from Exeter to Lyme, a little to the eastward of Sidford. The hill, which begins at this junction, is called Trow Hill, and on the top of it, towards the sea, lies *Trow,* a village of six or seven houses.

Knole, or *Knowl,* a house charmingly situated in a small luxuriant valley on the north of Trow Hill, a good view of which is to be obtained from a gate at the top, has long been the property and residence of the Woolcotts. *Slade House,* placed at the head of a most beautiful and richly wooded vale, commands a delightful view of the sea: it was built by the late William Leigh, Esq. and is now the residence of his widow and family: the estate formerly belonged to the Michells of Salcombe. Salcombe Church, a small edifice, but built upon a handsome model, is dedicated to St. Peter, whose image, with the usual insignia of the keys, appears on the outside of the chancel window. There is a room adjoining the church, called the Chapel, which was, probably, a place of worship before the church was built.

In this church not many monumental inscriptions remain.

Over a pew in the middle aisle, opposite to the pulpit, is a mural monument, which was long since erected to the memory of the family of Michell, of Slade, in this parish. On this monument are the arms of *Michell* impaling those of *Rotce,* and the inscription has been continued, and includes the date of the death of Captain Thomas Michell, the last male of the name, on the 8th of September, 1785, by his only nephew, Isaac Heard, Garter Principal King of Arms.

This family of Michell, previously to their removal to Slade, resided for nearly two centuries in a mansion called " *Sea-side House,"* within the parish of Branscombe, (now a farm-house belonging to Lady Rolle, and tenanted by Mr. Bartlett:) its situation is salubrious, beautiful, retired, and luxuriant, and near the sea. There is an interesting tradition in the family, which has been conveyed to us by a respectable authority, viz. That when James Duke of Monmouth landed at Lyme, in June 1685, a great number of people followed him and his party; many from ignorance, many from curiosity, and doubtless some, perhaps many, from dislike to the government of King James II. After the defeat of the Duke at Sedgemore, the west of England was subjected to the most wanton ravages of military tyranny, under the orders of Feversham and his followers. The savage Kirke became the executioner of numbers at and in the vicinity of Bridgewater; and the inhuman and infamous Jefferies followed, to complete, by the rigours of the law, the work of destruction. Hundreds of poor, ignorant, and undesigning "rebels" (as they were called) were condemned to death by terrified juries, and their quarters hung up in terrorem in the different

cross-ways. Pomfret, in his Poem entitled "Cruelty" and "Lust," has pathetically described the monster Kirke!

According to the tradition abovementioned, a number of these unfortunate persons, informed against for having been seen among Monmouth's followers, yet wholly innocent as to any overt-act of rebellion, or intention of committing any offensive acts, were sheltered in a cavern, or secret recess or recesses, on the sea-shore, near to Sea-side House, the mansion of the Michells, and supported with provisions by John Michell, Esq. the great-grandfather of Sir Isaac Heard, and his wife, during several weeks, or, at least, until the fury of the judge and executioners, and the rigour of the government under James, had begun to subside.

. The above-mentioned John Michell (who was a steady adherent of the royalist party) paid £140. as a composition for his estate, as appears by a list of the nobility, clergy, and gentry, who compounded for their estates in Devonshire in 1655. The estate was afterwards wrested from him by the violence of the times, but re-purchased—yet he met rather better treatment than many others;—for William Tsack, of Gittisham, Esq. father of his wife Joan, was considered to be a strong adherent of the Cromwellian interest. This John Michell died in 1710, aged 80—his wife Joan, the sole daughter and heir of the said William Isack, in September, 1730, aged 100—and Ursula Michell, his mother, whose family name was Drake, died in 1690, aged also 100. These three persons were buried in Branscombe Church; and their advanced ages may be adduced as some proof of the salubrity of the air in which they resided.

Bisdon says, " Salcombe is a place numbered amongst those which King Canute bequeathed to the church of St. Peter in Exeter, to expiate his father Swain's barbarous cruelty against the church in these parts." A neat modern parsonage-house, situated near the church, at the foot of a beautiful little hill, has a peculiarly snug and comfortable appearance.

The village itself consists of about

eight houses, including Coombe, a farm, about two-thirds pf the way between the church and the sea, and under delightful hanging woods, the residence of Mr. William Follett. Few places are more susceptible of improvement than this charming spot. Nature has done so much, that art has only to bestow a few embellishing touches: there is much to adorn, but nothing to create.

"England's Gazetteer," published in 1761, under the article " Salcombe," says, " In the civil wars, here was a fort, called Charles Fort, bravely defended against the Parliament forces, by Sir Edmund Fortescue, though he was at last forced to capitulate.

BRANSCOMBE

Lies east of Salcombe. This is a most romantic spot: the lofty cliffs which defend it from the sea, are, in many parts of it, paralleled at a small distance by inland hills, which abound with orchards, hanging woods, and enclosures, covered with grass or grain. Three vallies, forming a sort of triangle, meet near the church, which stands nearly in the middle of the parish. Through each of these vallies rapid streams descend, which, uniting in the bottom, flow on together to the ocean. Branscombe is separated from Beer by a small brook.

"It coasteth the sea," says Risdon, "and is full of coombes and vallies."

In Weston, a village of four farm houses, all but one of which are in ruins, John Stuckey, Esq. some years ago erected a handsome mansion: the old mansion and estate descended to him by inheritance; by him it was bequeathed to its present possessor, J. Bartlet Stuckey, Esq.

Edge, or *Egge,* in this parish, situated on an oval hill, was the dwelling-place of Ttichard Branscombe, in the reign of Edward III. It soon afterwards came to Sir John Wadham, the Judge; who, though remarkable for fluency of speech, never talked but with gravity and discretion, and who tempered all his words and actions with spirit and judgment. His reputation as a lawyer was very high. To his original estates he made many additions, among which was the rich manor of Silverton. He died in the reign of Henry IV. and was most probably buried in the family vault in Branscombe Church. The family of Wadham, who derived their name from the place of their origin and habitation, Wadham, near South Molton, possessed *Edge* for *eight* descents, in a direct line, *Jive* of whom were knights. The last of the family, Nicholas Wadham, of Edge, married Dorothy, the daughter of Sir William Petre. Having no issue, his sister's children became his heirs; but as he had made a very large addition to his patrimony, he determined to lay it out in founding a college. To him, therefore, and Dorothy his wife, Oxford is indebted for the foundation and establishment of *Wadham College.*

Branscombe Church, dedicated to St. Winifred, supposed to have been a native of Devonshire, is larger than St. Peter's, at Salcombe. It contains some monuments: on that erected to the memory of John Wadham, "time," says Prince, "hath rendered somewhat imperfect the following inscription:

"Here lieth intombed the body of a virtuous and ancient gentlewoman, descended of the ancient house of the Plantagenets, sometime of Cornwall, namely Joan, one of the daughters and heirs unto John Tregarthin in the county of Cornwall, Esq. She was first married unto John Kellaway, Esq. who had by her much issue: after his death, she was married to John Wadhani, of Merifield, in the county of Somerset, Esq. and by him had children. She lived a virtuous and godly life, and died in an honourable age, September in the year of Christ 1581." BEER

Is a small place, lying between very steep hills, about a mile from *Seaton.* Many of the houses are built of free-stone, from the famous free-stone quarry. The *Cove* is well calculated for fishing, and, from its situation, capable of being made one of the be3t fishing-places of the kingdom. Great quantities of fish are caught and brought in here; but a much larger quantity is sent off, by contract, to the markets of Taunton and Bath, and some even to London.

The classic author of the "Fisher Boy," a peculiarly faithful descriptive

Poem, lately published, has, in a note, some very just remarks, which are applicable, not only to the sea-scenery of Beer, but to various other parts of the coast.

"I have frequently repaired with a party of friends, to dine on some rocky eminence, bearing the cold provisions on a donkey. Upon such occasions, the cloth being spread on the grass, we have enjoyed a meal, surrounded by a grandeur of scenery that bade defiance to the most sumptuous edifices reared by the hand of art. From the madning height the expanded bosom of the ocean has reflected various colours; sometimes showing the red hue of the cliff lowering a darkening shade on the deep, at others, tinged with variegated hues of green, or spangled by the dazzling rays of a sultry sun. In short, all the varieties of prismatic colour have blazed in succession, a never-ending source of wonder and delight. As to inland scenery, I will allow that it is fraught with beauty, but for the truly sublime, nothing can vie with the surface of the ocean, whether in a calm, or agitated by tempestuous fury." *JSovey,* a very ancient seat in this manor, was the inheritance of the Walronds, of Bradfield, near Collumpton. It is at present the property of Lady Rolle, the only surviving daughter of the late William Walrond, Esq. It is a very old, irregular building, of free-stone. "The chapel here," says Risdon, "should seem to be founded by the Walronds, as their arms are cut in the moorstone pillars, just at the bottom of the arches."— "On visiting Bovey some years since," says a gentleman, "I was pleased with the venerable appearance of the house, and every object around it. It was then the residence of the widow of Mr. Walrond, just mentioned. There was something unusually striking in the antique mansion, the old rookery behind it, the mossy pavement of the court, the raven in the porch, grey with years, and even the domestics hoary in service— they were all grown old together."

The parish church is dedicated to St. Gregory. It is an ancient free-stone building, slated: the tower low and heavy, containing four bells. A hand-

some marble monument in the church bears the following inscription:

Sacred to the memory of William Walrond, Esq. who died at Bovey, in 1762, aged forty-five years; and of his first wife and infant son: also of Sarah Oke, his second wife, by whom he had issue, Sarah, Courtenay-William, and Judith-Maria. Of these, the last, alid only surviving one, wife of John Rolle, Esq. M. P. for Devon, erected this monument in respect of the best of parents, and at the request of her mother, who departed this life, February the 1st, 1787, aged 67."

The vicarage-house, near the church, is an old building. In this parish is one dissenting chapel. On an eminence, called *South Down,* is a most delightful and extensive prospect, by sea, from Portland, to the Start Point—by land, of a great part of the counties of Dorset, Somerset, and Devon. The chief employment of the inhabitants here and at Seaton is fishing, in which they are very expert. They are reckoned together, in both parishes, about fifteen hundred, in general strong and healthy. At the head of Beer, a pure spring rises out of the flint rock, and runs in a clear current through the town.

SEATON

Is a small town, "lying full upon the sea," irregularly built, and consisting chiefly of one street. Its situation is low and marshy; its hedges are well wooded; its roads are narrow, but good, and give scope for very pleasant walks and rides; its beach, though not so fine as that at Sidmouth, affords an agreeable promenade.

This place is memorable for the landing of the Danish princes in the year 937; as also for the attempt of the inhabitants of Colyton to make a port there, which they gravely named *Colyton Haven,* and procured a collection under the great seal of England, for the levying of money to effect their purpose: "Of this work," says Risdon, "there remains no monument," nor is the spot known where it was intended to be. On Seaton beach, as upon most of the openings of the coast, a small battery has been erected.

Salcombe, Branscombe, Beer, and Seaton, are all on the coast, and lie to the *south* of the road from Sidmouth to Lyme: the only places to the *north* of it, which our plan leads us to point out, are Colyton and Shute.

COLYTON,

Nine miles from Sidmouth, and about a mile to the north of Colyford, a small village, through which runs the turnpike road from Sidmouth to Lyme, is a small market town, situated on the western side of the Coly, where it falls into the Axe. It is a compact little place, and has a good market-house, a school-house, and a neat Presbyterian chapel. A large house, become by exchange of lands and inheritance the property of Sir William De la Pole, is the most considerable building in the place. The situation of Colyton is most delightful, lying in a beautiful and fertile valley, through which the Coly and the Axe roll their winding streams to the sea. The views from many parts in the vicinity of the town are extremely beautiful, being finely varied by a mixture of hill, vale, river, and sea. The enclosures are high hedges, planted in general with elm-trees. The houses are, for the most part, built of free and flint stone, and very neatly thatched. Colyton is a good dairy parish, remarkable for its rich butter and its " skim-milk" cheeses. The town, in the time of William the Conqueror, belonged to the Crown. Richard I. gave it, together with Whitford, to Thomas Basset, nephew of

F2

Walter Dunstanvil. King John granted an annual fair to continue eight days.

The church, dedicated to St. Andrew, is a strong stone edifice. The tower, which altogether looks handsome, consists apparently of one tower built upon another; the upper part is octagonal, raised on a large square structure that divides the church from the chancel. In this tower are six bells. On the southern side of the chancel is an enclosed burial-place, belonging to the De la Poles, highly ornamented with statues and other monumental decorations. In an enclosed burial-place, the property of Sir George Yonge's family, on the northern

side of the chancel, there is a small font for holy water. Under a stone canopy, in a small northern aisle, is the image of a girl, apparently about five years old. Over her are the Royal and the Courtenay arms. She is said to have been a grand-daughter of Edward *IV.* by one of his daughters, who was married to a Courtenay of Colcombe. Her death being, as was reported, occasioned by a fish-bone sticking in her throat, she is vulgarly called "the little choke-a-bonc. "

A new chapel, belonging to Dissenters, of Calvinistic sentiments, has been lately erected at Colyton; the pulpit originally in the church, was formerly occupied by Dr. Manton, whose ponderous volume of sermons on the 119th Psalm is said to have had considerable influence in making the celebrated Lord Shaftesbury an unbeliever.

Shute, a small parish, contains the village of *Whitford,* on the western side of the Axe: it consists of about twenty houses. A great part of a very old seat called *Shute House* was destroyed by its late owner, and a handsome modern habitation erected upon a larger scale. New Shute House, begun in 1787, is distant from the some of which is still visible. The jail was removed from thence to Bicton by the family of the Rolles, and thence to Exeter, where it now remains.

The church, a small low building, with a tower and three bells, is dedicated to St. Gregory. The vicarage house is a convenient modern edifice, erected in 1768.

Leaving Harford a little on the right hand, and crossing the Otter, over a stone bridge of five arches, the *Factory,* erected some years ago, for spinning of wool, strikes the eye as a very neat building. It stands on the left hand of the road, on the banks of the river, and is an ornamental feature in the beautiful scenery with which it is accompanied.

NEWTON POPPLEFORD

Is a long, mean-looking place, containing two public houses, dignified with the name of inns. Tradition says it was anciently a borough, though the charter has been long lost. It still retains its

portreeve. About the middle of the village is a chapel, lately repaired, dedicated to St. Luke. It was formerly a chantry, founded in the fourth year of Edward III. by Hugh de Courtenay, Earl of Devon. Tradition says it was built as an atonement for some crime. The commissioners in 1648, under the Commonwealth, remark—" Newton Poppleford, fit to be united to Harpford. Service every fifth Sunday at Newton." There is a large fair for cheese and cattle held here in October.

The Protestant Dissenters of *Calvinistic* sentiments are now erecting a chapel at Newton, nearly in the centre of the place.

CLYST ST. MARY,

Nearly twelve miles from Sidmouth, has nothing to distinguish it but a fine situation: it lies upon the river Grindle, which washes the western end of it. The length of the bridge marks the extent to which this stream sometimes inundates the meadows on each side. In 1748, there were seventeen families in St. Mary Clyst; in 1791, eighteen families, making a sum total of one hundred and seven persons. The Mansion-house is a large square white building, standing on an elevated spot, in a lawn of about sixty acres. The church of Clyst has nothing remarkable in it.

OTTERY ST. MARY,

Seven miles from Sidmouth, is the principal place to which the Otter, on which it stands, communicates its name:—it is a market town, and though built chiefly on a gentle hill, lies low with respect to the country through which it is approached. Dr. Maton, speaking of his ride to it from Sidmouth, says—" Taking leave of the coast for the present, we proceeded towards Exeter, through Ottery. The red oxyde of iron continued to tinge the soil the whole way, and added to the richness of the surrounding scenery; and the romantic winding of the river and the road exhibited a novel and agreeable effect. We descended into Ottery under the umbrage of widely spreading trees, the branches of which screened the town from our view until we arrived close to it; but the venerable towers of the church sometimes eeped through the foliage."

A clear stream runs through the town, and there are many convenient dipping-places from which the water may be easily taken: in the middle of the town is a spring, which sparkles with all the transparency of the Bristol waters, and is said to possess their qualities, but it has not their warmth. Another spring, rising near a house called Paradise, has been used medicinally as a solvent for the stone, and it was thought, by one gentleman, with some success.

The country about Ottery has all the features and beauties of the Devonshire landscape: the orchards and gardens, the verdure of the fields, and the richness of the hedge rows, at a little distance, form, from the line terrace in the church-yard, a very interesting picture. *j*

The houses in Ottery are strikingly various: in Mill Street is an old house, of a monasterial air, which was once the residence of the celebrated Sir Walter Raleigh. Cromwell's *Convention-room* is the largest of the parlours in one of the old collegiate houses, just by the church-yard.

These, and other edifices more or less ancient, are contrasted with the new brick houses erected after the fire, and the Factory, a new structure of considerable size. Of the fact connected with Cromwell's Convention-room, *Echard* gives the following account: "About the time that Exeter was besieged, Cromwell came to Ottery, to raise men and money from the town and neighbourhood. For this purpose he held a convention there, in a parlour now standing westward of the church. The people of Ottery refused to comply with his request, or rather requisition. Cromwell was so much irritated at their refusal, that he ordered his men to destroy all the ornaments of the church. The organ in the body of the church, and the organ in the chapel (now the library), were both dashed to pieces; and several fine monumental figures decapitated."

The church was dedicated and given to St. Mary in Roan by Edward the Confessor. "This church," says llisdon, "is fair according to the structure of those

times; whereof the windows, little and low, are so bedecked with the armories of diverse benefactors, more especially of the founders, that instead of *luxfuit,* it may be verified, that they are umbrated thereby." The two" towers, on the north and south sides, are, "each of them, it is said, eighty feet high, about half the height of those of Exeter cathedral, from which they were copied." By the style of the windows, it is supposed that these towers were erected about the time of Henry III.

This church has now a very handsome altar-piece; over which is inscribed *Jacobus Rex,* 1688. On the sides of the pulpit, which is of cedar, are admirably carved, by William Culne, a common carpenter, born in Ottery, the four Evangelists. In the body of the church, between two pillars, under a pyramidal arch, is the stone statue of a warrior, armed cap-a-pie, with a lion at his feet—and opposite, between two pillars, and arched in the same manner, is laid a female figure. Heraldic ornaments, now defaced by time, were once about these figures. There is no inscription, and tradition bestows upon them the names of William Grandison, father of the bishop, and Sibyl his wife:—in the chancel are several monumental inscriptions, in memory of the now decayed Haydon family, and others. The Calvinistio Dissenters have a chapel, and a considerable congregation in Ottery.

RIDE FROM SIDMOUTH, WESTWARD, OVER PEAK HILL.

To the westward of Sid mouth, between that and Exmouth, lie the following places, affording boundaries for longer or shorter excursions; *Otterton, Bicton, Woodbury, Budleigh, Salterton,* and *Littleham.* Several of these places can be seen from Peak Hill, particularly Otterton and Bicton.

OTTERTON,

That is, *a town upon the Otter,* is now a poor place, consisting principally of one street. The male inhabitants of it are almost entirely farmers and their labourers, with a few necessary mechanics: the females are almost wholly employed in the making a coarse kind of

thread lace. The situation of the parish is both pleasant and healthy. The cliffs bordering on the sea are very high, and nearly perpendicular: the air is dry and salubrious: a stone bridge crosses the river: the roads are very narrow: the enclosures are numerous; and the orchards and hedges very flourishing. Camden says, "the name of the river is derived from the plenty of *otters* or water-dogs. " Modern observation does not confirm this account, whatever it might have been formerly; the *Otter* is now merely a *trout-stream.*

The manor of Otterton is a very noble one. From the conquest to the dissolution of abbies, it continued in the hands of religious men. William the Conqueror gave it to *St. Michael de Monte,* in Normandy. Upon the surrender, Richard Duke, a clerk of the Augmen

G tation-court, procured it, and built a noble house upon an ascent a little way from the river, which turns the mills below. The grant, dated in 1540, gives to Richard Duke the manors of Otterton and East Budleigh, with all their rights and privileges, and royalties, and the patronage of the vicarages of Otterton, Budleigh, and Harpford, for the sum of *e61727.* 4s. 2d.

In 1775 the Duke estate, in default of male heirs, descended to four sisters, now all dead. Soon after the estate was advertised for sale. Lord Rolle was the purchaser, and is the present possessor of it: he has taken down almost the whole of the house.

Close to the remains of the house stands the church, dedicated to St. Michael, a stone building, with a slated roof: within it is extremely neat, being uniformly pewed with the best wainscot, at the recommendation of Mr. John Duke, about fifty years ago. The inhabitants of Otterton House were, for several ages, much inclined to the Dissenting cause.

Crossing Otterton Bridge, at a little distance on the right hand, lies BICTON,

The property and residence of Lord Rolle, who has lately completed a noble mansion, which may be seen from Peak Hill. It stands in a beautiful park, well stocked with deer, and distinguished for its noble and venerable groves of beech and oak. It is remarkable, that the tenure of Bicton is still to keep the jail of the county. "This," it has been remarked, "is perfectly right: the possessor of the manor of Bicton has been always obliged" (from the time of Henry I.) "*to find a county jail*"

The church of Bicton, dedicated to the Holy Trinity, is thus beautifully described by the historian of Devonshire. "It is a small, but neat building. Its situation is most romantic. Placed in silence and solitude, it stands embowered amidst the fine deep foliage of forest trees, that surround it at a little distance, and interweave their branches, as if to secure it from every prying eye. Whilst we approach the church, we feel sensations of awe, from its *holy* seclusion: but they are mixed with ideas of fairy scenery. The spot is, in itself, most enchanting. Thus encircled by such a beautiful screen of woods, thus insulated, and withdrawn from the world, we fancy ourselves amidst the groves of Rousseau's Ermenonville, and recalling his fine painting to memory, can recognize, almost, its prototype in the objects around us."

The present parsonage-house, a convenient brick mansion, was built about forty years ago: it stands on a rising ground, about a quarter of a mile from the church, and in full view of the public road.

BUDLEIGH.

There are two or three villages of this name, at no great distance from each other. The church, and a Dissenting chapel, stand in the principal one, denominated East Budleigh, through which lies the road from Sidmouth to Salterton, and to Exmouth. Sir W. Pole says, "Budleigh is a small market town. " The church is dedicated to All Saints: it is a handsome stone edifice, with a square tower eighty feet high: it has five bells and a clock. There are several coats of arms in the windows, and on the facing of the old seats. On one seat is a representation of Bishop Blaze. In the

G 2 church yard is a stone with this inscription, but without a date: *Orate*

pro anima Radulphi Node.
"Pray for the soul of Radulphus Node."

Tradition says, this was the sepulchre of a man who broke his neck in attempting to fly from the church tower with artificial wings: the inscription, it seems, is now obliterated.

TIDWELL HOUSE

Is a large, square, and remarkably substantial brick building, with a multitude of windows, at a small distance from the road to Exmouth. It had formerly lords so named. *Joan,* the daughter of the last of that line, was the wife of *John de St. Clere.* Gabriel St. Clere, one of his descendants, after he had wasted his estate, by excessive hospitality, began to take his house to pieces, and sell the materials; affirming, that "neither he nor his posterity could prosper, as long as one stone stood upon another, of a house where so many sins had been committed." One of this family, we are told, was distinguished by the following act of uncommon loyalty: When Henry II. was besieging the castle of Bridgnorth, in the possession of Hugh de Mortimer, Hubert de St. Clere, perceiving the King aimed at from the castle walls, stepped in before his sovereign, received the arrow into his own body, and expired. The King not only interred the deceased with all military honours, but took his young and only daughter under his protection; and when she was marriageable, gave her to William de Longville, a man of noble birth, and in high favour with the King. With her, the inheritance descended from her father, with large additions; but on these terms—" that, to perpetuate the memory of the faithful Hubert, Longville should bear both the name and surname of her father, and be called Hubert de St. Clere. The present house was built by Counsellor Walrond about seventy years ago, and is now, in right of his wife, the property of John Edye, Esq. of Pinney, near Lyme. Of the springs at Tidwell, Risdon gives the following account: "The ponds at Tidwell, maintained by springs, continually whelm and boil up, not unlike that wonderful well in Derbyshire, which ebbeth and floweth by just tides. These springs are

so warm, that, whilst all the waters around them are frozen, they are free from ice in the coldest weather; when abundance of wildfowl flock hither, to the no little pleasure and profit of the place." *Hays,* situated on the western side of the parish of East Budleigh, is celebrated as the birth-place of the famous Sir Walter Raleigh.

The general history of this celebrated man is too well known to be here recapitulated: the peculiar severity, not to say injustice, of the sentence by which he was at last executed, gives him a claim to the compassion of all succeeding ages, and serves to immortalize a name which, both by the pen and the sword, has become dear to his country.

In the Fourth Book of the Columbiad, an epic poem, of considerable merit, which has recently made its appearance, the following just and animated picture of this great man occurs: "High on the tallest deck majestic, shone

Sage Raleigh, pointing to the western sun:

His eye, bent forward, ardent and sublime,

Seem'd piercing nature, and evolving time:

Beside hira stood a globe, whose figures trac'd

A future empire in each present waste;

All former works of men behind him shone,

Grav'd by his hand in ever-during stone:

On his calm brow a various crown displays

The hero's laurel and the scholar's bays;

His graceful limbs in steely mail were drest,

The bright star beaming on his lofty breast;

His sword, high waving, flash'd the solar ray,

Illum'd the shrouds, and rainbow'd far the spray;

The smiling crew rose resolute and brave,

And the glad sails hung bounding o'er the wave."

'.' The Aubrey Papers," published in 1813, contain the following account of this celebrated man:

"Sir Walter Raleigh was a tall, handsome, bold man—he had a most remarkable aspect, an exceeding high forehead, long faced, and sour eye-lidded, a kind of a pig-eye. He was the first that brought tobacco to England and into fashion. In Malmsbury Hundred, in North Wiltshire it came first into fashion, by Sir Walter Long. They had first silver pipes. Common people used a walnut-shell and a straw. I have heard my great-grandfather Lyte say, that one pipe was handed from man to man round the table. Sir Walter Raleigh, standing in a stand at Sir Robert Poyntz's park at Acton, took a pipe of tobacco, which made the ladies quit it till he had done. For a long time it was scandalous for a divine to take tobacco. I have heard some of our old yeomen neighbours say, that when they went to Malmsbury or Chippenham market, they culled out their biggest shillings to lay in the scales against the tobacco. I have heard my cousin Whitney say, that he saw Sir Walter in the Tower. He had a velvet cap, laced, a rich gown, and trunk hose.

In his speech on the scaffold, he spake not one word of Christ, but of the great and incomprehensible God, with much zeal and adoration, so that my cousin Whitney concluded he was an *a-christ,* not an *atheist."* "Old Sir Thomas Malett, one of the justices of the King's Bench in the time of Charles I. and II. knew Sir Walter, and I have heard him say, that, notwithstanding his so great mastership in style, and his conversation with the learnedst, and politest persons, yet he spake broad Devonshire to his dying day. His voice was small."

"Sir W. Raleigh's letter to Mr. Duke, in Devon, writ with his own hand. "Mr. Duke,

"I wrote to Mr. Prideaux to move you for the purchase of *Hay's,* a farm sometime in my father's possession. I will most willingly give whatsoever in your conscience you shall deem it worth, and if at any time you shall have occasion to use me, you shall find me a thankful friend to you and yours. I am resolved, if I cannot entreat you, to build at Colliton; but for the natural disposition I have to that place, being born in that house, I had rather seat myself there than any where else. I take my leave, readic to countervaile all your courtesies to the utter of my power.

"Your very willing friend,

"In all that I shall be able,

"WALTER RALEGH."

"Court, July 26,1584." BUDLEIGH SALTERTON,

Two miles from East Budleigh, is a small village upon the coast, lying in sight of Torbay; it is increasing in reputation as a watering-place, and the number of its lodging-houses has been greatly augmented in the last few years. Its beach, by the side of which a narrow walk has been constructed, is distinguished by a vast multitude of broad, flat, oval-shaped pebbles, some of which are veined in a curious manner.

A small chapel, in which the worship of the church of England is performed, has been built by Lord Rolle; and by the late Mr. Lackington, a handsome chapel for the Wesleyan Methodists, the present minister of which is the worthy and eloquent Mr. Hawtrey.

From Saltcrton, a pleasant road leads the traveller to LITTLEHAM,

A small village, two miles from Exmouth, and in the parish of which Exmouth lies. Its church is dedicated to the Holy Trinity, and lies under a hill called Westdown. "Here, in an aisle belonging to the Drake family," says Prince, "is this epitaph, on the tomb of Robert Drake," who was noticed for his benefactions in the time of Charles I.

Preachers and poor can say my death
Was ended in a lively faith;
The yearly gifts that I then gave
Till time be ended they must have.

This Robert Drake, born at *Sprathays,* in the parish of Littleham, was the third son of Gilbert Drake, of that place, a younger branch of the family of Ash. After having studied the law at the Inner Temple, he married and settled at *Daleditch,* in East Budleigh. He died in 1638.

EXMOUTH

Is the oldest watering-place in Devonshire. Prince calls it " a small hamlet." About a century ago, one of the judges of the circuit, in a very infirm state of health, received so much benefit from bathing there, that it was brought into repute. It is ten miles south from Exeter, and the same from Sidmouth. It is sheltered from the north-east and south-east winds by some hills, which supply it with excellent water. It is now a considerable place, and can boast a great many new and commodious houses.

A part of a letter, written about thirty years ago, giving an account of what Exmouth was then, is here inserted, because it serves to mark more distinctly the numerous improvements which have since taken place, not only there, but in all the watering-places on the coast: at that time Exmouth was, probably, at the head of the list.

"The village is a very pretty one, and composed for the most part of cot-houses, neat and clean, consisting of four or five rooms, which are generally let at a guinea a-week. We have, from some of the houses, when the tide is in, a beautiful view of the river, which, united with the sea, forms a fine sheet of water before our doors, of large extent. Lord Courtenay and Lord Lisburne's grounds, rising in inequalities on the other shore, complete the perspective. This is the most gay part of the village: but then its brilliancy is only temporary; for, the tide returned, instead of a fine sheet of water, we are presented with a bed of mud, whose perfumes are not exactly those of a bed of roses. Another part affords you the view of scattered cottages, forming a pleasing rural scene. Here the gratification which the eye receives is less delightful and more durable; for which last property there are some who prefer this to the former situation. Exmouth boasts no public rooms nor assemblies, save one card assembly, in an incpnvenient apartment, at one of the inns, on Monday evenings. The company meet at halfpast five, and break up at ten: they play at shilling whist, and two-penny quadrille. We have very few young people here, and no diversions. Walking on a hill which commands a view of the ocean, and bathing, with a visit or two, serve to pass away the morning, and tea-drinking in the evening."—It is necessary here to remark what a different picture is here delineated from that to which we are now witnesses? Is it worth while to decide upon which is the best? *Tempora mutanhtr, et mutamur cum Mis.* "Say not," says the Wise man, "that the former days were better than these; for thou dost not enquire wisely concerning this."

At Exmouth, Risdon tells us, was born Sir Richard Whitebourne, Knight, whose adventurous voyages in discovering the commodities of Newfoundland, and endeavours for the plantations and profitable fishings there, have merited the general commendation of his country, and received honour of the King. From hence the Earl of March, afterwards Edward IV. accompanied with the Earls of Sarum and Warwick, set sail for Calais, anno 1459, by the assistance of John Dynham, Esq. afterwards Lord Treasurer of England.

A New Library has lately been opened at Exmouth, and other improvements made.

LYMPSTONE,
Ten miles from Sidmouth, the road from which runs through Otterton, and by Bicton Park, is delightfully situated on the east side of the Exe. It is very irregularly built; good houses and mean cottages, are in the middle of it, rather closely huddled together. At the end of the village is the church, which is seen to advantage, as it stands at a little distance from the road. Directly opposite the road are some fine meadows, through which lies a pleasant rural walk to the hamlet of Sowdon: this path winds delightfully by the side of willows, or amidst clumps of lofty elms, to a charmingly neat and rural spot, where are some decent lodgings, with gardens and orchards about them. Fishing and lacemaking are the employments of the inhabitants of this place.

The church is dedicated to St. Mary. It is rather low in proportion to the tower, which contains five musical bells. On the glass of a window, in the north aisle, St. George is represented, with this inscription: . the holy Knight,

Who slew the dragon by his might.

This church is well seated, and has a handsome altar-piece. A neat Dissenting chapel stands just within Woodbury parish: the attendants are chiefly from Lympstone, where the minister resides.
WOODBURY,
So called from its *ancient woodlands,* is a parish with eight villages, and still abounding with oak, elm, and ash. Woodbury Castle, which crowns the extensive common of that name, gives a noble effect to the prospect.
Church Village is nearly in the centre of the parish. The church, which was new-built, and dedicated to St. Swithin, in 1409, is an edifice of durable stone, with a slated roof, and is twenty feet high. The tower, which is eighty feet, is square, has two strong but" tresses at each corner, and on the top sixteen battlements, and a weathercock. It contains six deep-toned musical bells. In the church is one monument, without an inscription, erected in memory of the present Sir Wilmot Prideaux's ancestors, who lived at *Nutwell,* the seat of Sir Francis Drake, so distinguished in the naval records of England.
Exmouth, Lympstone, Topsham, Lyme, and Axminster, are all too far from Sidmouth, to be often visited from thence. It has, however, been thought that this picture would scarcely be complete without some slight notice of these places, which lie, as it were, upon the frame in which it is enclosed. For the same reason, Exeter might claim a description; this, however, is wholly declined, as it would be impossible to do any thing like justice to the Metropolis Of The West, without too much increasing the bulk of this publication. With a brief account, therefore, of Topsham, Lyme, and Axminster, this little work will conclude. TOPSHAM
Consists principally of, one street, about half a mile tang, one part of which is considerably wider than the other. Many good houses are scattered through the town, but upon the whole it has but a mean appearance. The southern end is by far the pleasantest part; it is called the *Strand,* and is inhabited mostly by people out of trade. It commands a fine view of the river and the

opposite bank. A little further up is the *Quay,* which is large, and now belongs to the corporation of Exeter. The road from Topsham to Exeter is very good, and rendered extremely pleasant by several detached genteel houses, and ornamented gardens and lawns on each side.

The church has an antique appearance; it is a large but tasteless building, dedicated to *St. Margaret.*— It stands on the edge of a high cliff, and consequently commands a more extensive view than the Strand. This prospect is full of beauty,—a noble river—distant shipping—church-towers glimmering through groupes of trees—a fertile vale, and a fine range of mountains rising one above another, as far as the eye can reach. Besides the church, Topsham has three places of worship, two belonging to the Dissenters, and one to the Quakers.

The *Retreat,* formerly a sugar-house, but now a highly ornamented mansion, is perhaps the best residence in the immediate vicinity of Topsham.
LYME,
Sixteen miles from Sidmouth, is a small sea-port town in Dorsetshire: it has long been known as a watering-place. It is situated close to the sea, at the mouth of a narrow valley, the sides of which are high and steep hills: it is an old place, as the appearance of many of the houses sufficiently proves. The public room for the company is lofty and spacious, and looks full upon the bay in which the town stands. A public walk is constructing near the sea, but the shore does not admit of its at all rivalling the beach at Sidmouth; and when the tide is out, the quantity of mud which is left behind is grateful neither to the optic or olfactory nerves.,

The peculiarity of Lyme is the *Pier,* which forms its port, and which is denominated the *Cobb.* Within this solid enclosure of masonry, vessels lie in perfect security, but the entrance is narrow, and in stormy weather difficult to hit. The walk upon it, however, which is broad, and faced with durable stone, is, at all times, when it is dry, and the wind not too boisterous, extremely pleasant.

The liberties of a haven and borough

were granted to Lyme by Edward I., and from this period it grew so prosperous, that in the reign of Edward III. it furnished four ships and sixty-two mariners, for the siege of Calais. The corporation consists of a mayor, recorder, town-clerk, and fifteen capital burgesses. It has sent representatives to Parliament eve'r since the twenty-third of Edward I. The number of houses returned under the population act in 1803, was two hundred and seventy-six; the inhabitants one thousand four hundred and fifty-one.

The siege of Lyme, during the civil wars, was one of the most remarkable which took place during that calamitous period.

Captain *Thomas Coram,* the patron and contriver of the Foundling Hospital, was born at Lyme in 1668: in his benevolent attention to others, this singularly humane and memorable man so entirely forgot himself, that in his old age he was supported by a pension of somewhat more than a hundred pounds a-year, raised for him at the solicitation of Sir Sampson Gideon and Dr. Brocklesby. Upon Dr. Brocklesby's applying to him, to know whether a subscription being opened for his benefit would not offend him? he received this noble answer: "I have not wasted the little wealth of which I was formerly possessed in self-indulgence, or vain expences, and am not ashamed to confess, that in this my old age I am poor." He died at his lodgings near Leicester Square, March 29, 1751, eighty-three years old. "The memory of the *good* shall be blessed."

Between Lyme and Colyton, about two miles from the former place, lies *Finney,* an estate belonging to John Edye, Esq. who resides upon it—the grounds, especially upon the coast, are exceedingly romantic and picturesque.

Upon the hill, about half a mile from Lyme, George Holland, Esq. has lately built a large and tasteful villa, which he has named *High Cliff.* It Is furnished with great elegance, and possesses a spacious and magnificent music-room. The view of the ocean from this truly "marine villa," is peculiarly grand and impressive.

AXMINSTER,

Nine miles from Honiton, and five from Colyton, is a healthy clean town, in the road from Exeter to London: it lies on a little hill by the river Axet "whence," says Risdon, "it was so called, without any addition, till King Athelstan's time. But when at this place a *minster* was erected, wherein seven priests should pray for the souls of those that were slain, this place got that adjunct which it now holdeth." It anciently belonged to the kings of England.—From the heights in its neighbourhood the sea is to be discovered. "From the hill tops about Stockland," says Dr. Stukeley, "I first had sight of the Southern Ocean, a most solemn view, a boundless extent of water, thrown into a mighty horizontal curve."

The church, some parts of which have the appearance of great antiquity, has a very heavy appearance, particularly on the inside—it is dedicated to St. Mary. There is a school-house close by the church, the windows of which are rounded in the Saxon style. The walk in the church-yard is pleasant, between rows of flourishing lime-trees. The Dissenters have a well-attended chapel in this town.

A durable sort of carpets, which somewhat resemble tapestry, and are called Axminster carpets, have long been manufactured here, and are generally esteemed.

As the first part of this little volume is closed by a sonnet to Sidmouth, the following elegant lines on " seabathing," which, though dated *Barmouth,* are by no means restricted to that place, may not unappropriated close the whole:

Freed from the conch of sickness, grief, and pain,

Hither the fainting sufferer comes to lave,

In the cool freshness of the bracing wave,

His languid limbs: If so, he may regain

The thousand blessings that compose the train

Of rosy health! and oh! if aught can save _

From the dark precincts of the gloomy grave,

Barmouth! 'tis thee, and all thy sylvan reign.

GENERAL INFORMATION. THE POST OFFICE. The Post arrives from Exeter every morning about nine o'clock, which conveys the letters from London put in two days previous. Letters for London or elsewhere must be put into this office by half after six, but by paying one penny with each letter they are received from that time till seven o'clock, when the bag is closed.

A COACH To and from Honiton now runs daily, and twice a-week, to Taunton, which it is hoped will meet sufficient encouragement to render it permanent, the convenience being found truly desirable. It carries four inside passengers—leaves Sidmouth in time to meet at Honiton the Bath and London coaches; it leaves Honiton every evening at half-past six, and arrives at Sidmouth between eight and nine. A new line will shortly be completed, by which will be avoided the old and dangerous road down Pin Hill.

CARRIERS.

John Way and ¥m. Cockram convey goods to and from Exeter every Monday, Wednesday, and Friday.

PLEASURE BOATS, Attended by expert and careful seamen, are always ready; the principal are kept by

J. and R. Bartlet, R. Puddicombe,
   Thomas Heffer, John Taylor,
   Henry Conant, R. Boult, &c.
   W. Radford and T. Silley,
   A two hours sail is charged 0 5 0
   To Exmouth and home 1 1 0
   To Dawlish or Teignmouth 11 6
   H SEDAN AND BATH CHAIRS
   Arc kept by "Win. Rugg, J. and R. Bartlet, W. Rad4 ford and T. Silley.

A GOOD HORSE AND GIG
is to be hired of Mr. Hall, Linen Draper. The principal persons who let horses, are—

   B. Butter Painter.
   Wm, Gove Druggist.
   Wm. Gale.Linen Draper.
   Matthew Hall....Linen Draper.,.
   Sam. Pile Cabinet Maker.
   J. Pester Baker.

W. Cawsey Painter, &c. t. s.
Henry Smith has quiet and manageable Donkies, with proper saddles for invalids; he also supplies Asses' Milk.
BATHING MACHINES
Kept by Marmaduke Taylor and Thomas Heffer, for Gentlemen.— Terms of bathing, One Shilling first time, and Sixpence each time after.

By Mrs. Barrett and Co. for Ladies. —One Shilling and Sixpence first time, aad Is. each time after.
APPENDIX.
Since the former part of this work was printed, a more particular account of one of the Charitable Institutions of Sidmouth, which is mentioned in page 40, has been obtained, and is as follows. It was established June 22, 1812, is supported by voluntary subscriptions, and is denominated Sidmouth School, for the Education of the Infant Poor, *in the Principles of the* Established Church, and according to Dr. Bell's plan.
Patron, Patroness, and Presidents.
The Rt. Hon. Lord Gwydir and Lady Willoughby.
Spiritual Governor,
The Vicar of Sidmouth for the time being.
Vice Presidents and Committee.
Lady Kennaway. Sir J. Kennaway, Bart.
Mrs. Jenkins. Sir Jos. Scott, Bart.
Mrs. Hobson. The Rev. J. Hobson.
Mrs. Powys Floyd. Rev. W. Jenkins, jun.
Mrs. Fulford. Geo. Cornish, Esq.
Mrs. Reynolds. E. B. Lousada, Esq.

Henry Cutler, Esq. *Treasurer,* Mr. John Newbery.
August 23,1814.—At a Meeting of the Subscribers, held at the School Room, it was resolved—..,.'..,
That this meeting see with considerable satisfaction the increasing utility of this institution, and are gratified at finding that nearly fifty children are now educating in the school. .-,"./ i..c." '.- ADDITIONAL BUILDINGS, &c.
Mrs. Floyd's new cottage is nearly completed; it consists wholly of a ground floor, and is arranged and decorated with that lady's peculiarly elegant and happy taste. The length of the building is 120 feet, the middle division of which is to be a conservatory. The name is *Forays Cottage*—it commands a fine view of the sea, and is surrounded with extensive and beautiful shrubberies and walks.
Major Sandford's cottage is finished in a style of great neatness, and the lane between his and Mrs. Floyd's premises is greatly improved and beautified.
General Baynes has purchased King's Cottage; added a part of the adjoining field to his grounds; made several judicious improvements, and given it the name of Woolbrook Cottage.
Mr. Denbigh has added a third house to the two he had before built in Fort Field, and inclosed the remaining part of his ground with a brick wall.
Numerous parcels of the manor have lately been disposed of to individuals; it is therefore anticipated still greater

improvements will present themselves within the year 1817. Other buildings in the Fort Field, it is said are projected; this delightful spot must ever maintain a preference, and continue the court-end of Sidmouth.
MASTERS.
Drawing—-Mr. H. Haseler, Member of Spring Gardens Society.
Music—Mr. Williams, Karp-master.
Teachers of Piano-forte.—Mr. Mudge and Mr.'Heather. i«.--,- '"--. —
Dancing—Mr. and Mrs. Mason.
Those who admire fine scenery will be amply gratified by the following rides near Sidmouth. Through Harpford "Wood; after which, ascend Ottery Hill to the ancient fire-beacon. Through the valley of Branscomb to the sea-shore; ride on the beach, to the eastward, half a mile, and view the cliffs; on your return, the view of Sidmouth Bay and Peak Cliffs will reward a ride to Dunscomb. The following places on the coast, *eastzcard,* are distant from Sidmouth—Charmouth, 18 miles; Lyme Regis, 16 miles; Seaton, 10 miles; Beer, 8 miles; Branscomb 6, Salcombe 2. *Westward—*Otterton, 3 miles; Budleigh Salterton, 6 miles; Lympstone, 9; Exmouth, 12 miles; Dawlish, lti miles; Teignmouth, 20 miles; Torquay, 25 miles. *Inland—*Exeter, 16 miles; Ottery, St. Mary, 7, Honiton, 9; Axminster, 16; Chudleigh, 26; Crediton, 25; Tiverton, 25; Collumpton, 18.

Lightning Source UK Ltd.
Milton Keynes UK
UKOW02f2355310114

225693UK00011B/456/P